I0463140

Dedication

For Heather, Mark, Brendan. and Clarissa

Acknowledgements

My good friend, Andrew Oravets, first showed me the significance of systematically supporting leadership transitions within organizations. His work on transitions at the Syntex Corporation and his insights as a Human Resources professional and executive coach have been a major influence on the work presented here. I am grateful to Larry Costello, Dave Pannier, Tom Schlegel, Bill Burgdorf, Becky Steph, Paul Fisher and Katherine Hartvickson for supporting my work at American Standard and the Trane Corporation where I was able to implement and refine the method provided by *Leadership Transitions Solutions* and described in this book. Bill Kramer of AT&T has been an important supporter of my work. Melanie Keveles and Karen McClaskey have helped me strengthen the services of my company and I appreciate their partnership in providing coaching services as an integral part of *Leadership Transitions Solutions*.

I also wish to acknowledge all of those executives who participated in my transition services and enabled me to continually improve their quality.

TABLE OF CONTENTS

Introduction

The last ten years in the global economy have made incessant change the only constant in the life of most every organization. The companies that have continued to grow and flourish in this setting are those that have implemented substantial change management techniques. During this time my professional focus has been on coaching senior leaders facing the challenge of a transition to a new assignment. The single most important understanding that I have taken from these ten years is this: *Successful leadership transitions require deep and sophisticated listening on the part of the leader at the very start of the new assignment.* It is the kind of listening required of a skilled physician taking the pulse of a patient. It is the kind of listening that should be a core element in the change management strategy of any company concerned with continual growth and increased profitability.

Taking the pulse is a core diagnostic procedure in the history of all of the world's medical traditions. In biomedicine it is the key to discerning the health of the heart of the human organism. Traditional Chinese Medicine (TCM) takes the pulse on both the right and left wrists and identifies 12 different results, each of which discerns the health of a particular organ in the body. In the Ayurvedic tradition the pulse identifies the status of the body's three basic energy types.

This is a book about a carefully refined method for leaders to take the pulse of an organization. The method enables the transitioning leader to engage in deep and sophisticated listening to the organization as an organism constantly in need of improvement. It describes what needs to be a core procedure for any leader assuming the challenge of a new assignment. The method enables the leader to efficiently master the new organization and thereby understand the specific actions that need to be taken to boost its productivity and profitability.

Leadership transitions are unrivalled opportunities for learning. Managers facing the challenge of a new assignment can develop new capacities of perception as a result of careful and thoughtful participation in the method presented here. Like the masterful physician diagnosing the needs of a patient, the transitioning leader can learn to listen deeply and quickly master the needs and challenges facing him. The same sharpening of perception can take place for the manager's new team and its individual members who participate in the process. In addition, every transition event can produce organizational learning and development. In order to realize these learning opportunities, it is necessary to plan and manage every transition by systematically applying the method described in the pages that follow.

The intent of this book is to describe all of the processes and resources required for consistently effective leadership transitions. Together these activities and resources constitute a sophisticated method for taking the pulse of the organization. The method ensures that the new leader will know precisely how to improve the health and productivity of the organization. The reader will also discover here resources and activities for Chief Learning Officers wanting to realize the learning opportunities inherent in leadership transitions, for HR executives looking for a method to systemically support transitions and for coaches and Transition Coach's focused on providing effective support to transitioning managers. The resources and program components described here are provided by *Leadership Transitions Solutions* to corporations. They have been developed and refined over the last ten years. They can also be customized to meet the needs of unique transitions.

After decades of work with major corporations, I have yet to find an organization that consistently realizes the learning potential inherent in leadership transitions by systematically applying the program elements described in the chapters that follow. Most major corporations claim to have programs in place, but they are almost never applied systematically and their quality varies dramatically by relying excessively on the individual competencies and experience of support personnel. And very few corporations are taking advantage of web-based applications like the one described here to support the generation of actionable intelligence for the transitioning manager, as well as for the organization. *Dialogue™* is the web-based application developed by LTS to support interviews with superiors, peers, direct reports and internal and external customers. It generates all of the intelligence needed to suppport a succesful startup for the newly appointed leader. These same applications are also a source of quality control because they provide efficient support mechanisms that do not rely on individual competencies and experience.

Chapter One addresses the transitioning manager directly and provides an orientation to a comprehensive leadership transition program. It is a workbook for the manager and is designed to ensure successful participation in the transition program and a successful startup in the new position. The chapter is a detailed description of a sophisticated method for taking the pulse of the organization in order to know what to do to improve its health and productivity. The role of *Dialogue™* is described in detail.

Chapter Two provides an actual case study of a manager participating in a comprehensive leadership transition program provided by *Leadership Transitions Solutions* to a major manufacturing corporation. The program utilizes the support of Dialogue™ , the web-based application developed by *Leadership Transitions Solutions* to gather intelligence by interviewing all of the key individuals surrounding a manager beginning a new assignment. This is followed by a description of an effective transition meeting. This meeting is facilitated by a transition coach who provides ongoing coaching support during the first three months in the new assignment.

Chapter Three describes a method for designing the Transition Meeting, including specific recommendations for effective facilitation of this meeting and use of the Transition Coach. The Transition Meeting enables the new manager to produce an effective action plan in collaboration with the new team of direct reports. It functions as a catalyst for the development of an effective relationship between the new manager and the team of direct reports. As the high-touch part of the method it complements the high-tech role of *Dialogue™*.

Chapter Four provides an actual summary report generated by *Dialogue™*, *Leadership Transitions Solutions*' web-based application that conducts interviews with direct reports, peers, superiors and customers prior to the Transition Meeting. It provides an example of the richness of information and intelligence that can be generated by the appropriate use of web-based technology in the leadership transition process.

Chapter Five provides a theoretical basis for the specific practices involved in an effective leadership transition program. It describes the effective use of web-based

8

applications in a strategic approach to creating a
learning culture, a culture that honors the nature of the adult
learner and realizes the potential of eLearning in today's
organizations. The chapter is specifically addressed to Chief
Learning and Chief Human Resources Officers .

Each chapter begins with an executive summary as a
guide to the efficient use of the book as a whole.

My hope is that this book will promote the more
systematic utilization of an effective leadership transition
process, one which capitalizes on all of the learning
opportunities inherent in every leadership transition event.
Developing leaders for today's organizations depends upon
the ongoing development of new capacities of perception in
individual leaders. There is no more practical way of doing
this than to install a carefully designed leadership transition
program and be wise enough to apply it systematically. Just
as a physician would not act on the human organism without
doing a skillful pulse taking, the leader in every transition
needs to apply the method described here before taking
action in the new assignment.

In today's global economy where incessant change is the
only constant, it is not unusual for a leader to experience
many transitions over the span of a career. Each transition
that involves careful pulse taking of the organization on the
part of the leader will increase the leadership competencies of
the individual involved. Like the master Chinese physician
who has learned great diagnostic and healing powers for the
human organism, the constantly growing leader will bring the
capacities of masterful leadership to each new assignment.

Chapter One: A Guide to Effectively Assuming a New Management Role

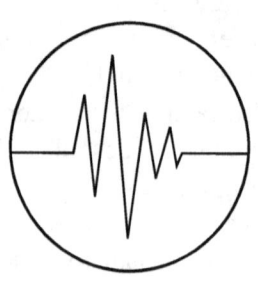

Executive Summary for Chapter One

This chapter is addressed directly to a manager facing the challenge of a new assignment. It provides an orientation to *Leadership Transitions Solutions'* leadership transition process and a guidebook for the transitioning manager. The challenges and characteristics of the transition process are identified, as well as the factors involved in failed transitions. It also identifies four key phases to the process:

1. Issue identification and goal clarification

2. Team development

3. Articulating vision, goals and agenda for the new organization

4. Developing an initial vision and agenda

The chapter presents some of the key questions that are part of the web-based interviews conducted by *Leadership Transitions Solutions* to produce a comprehensive assessment of the new organization. The *Dialogue™* application is designed to gather all of the information needed by the transitioning leader in a more efficient and systematic manner. It not only saves time, it also ensures all the bases are covered.

The Chapter also provides a set of self-assessment questions for the new manager to increase self-awareness and enhance learning during the transition process.

11

INTRODUCTION

A change in leadership within an organization may be compared to passing the baton in a relay race. The runner with the baton must maintain speed and momentum until the baton is passed, while the relief runner must come up to speed and continue the race. Both must take care that the baton is passed smoothly for the team to maintain its winning position. If the baton is dropped, the race is lost. If the pass is successful, the team's chances of winning are increased. In any leadership transition in a business organization, the relief runner is new and must learn the intricacies of the team: how they plan their business strategies and  tactics, execute them successfully, and celebrate those successes. The organization and the new leader must meld quickly into a high performing team. Particularly in functions with a wide variety of customers, stakeholders and complex responsibilities, managers need to know as much as possible about their new organization. The use of a planned transition process will significantly speed the organization's acceptance of the new manager as well as reduce the lost productivity often associated with a change of leadership. This is also a major opportunity for the personal and professional development of the individual. Hidden within the difficult disruptions usually connected with transition are invitations to real personal growth. By approaching the transition events with an openness to learning, the new manager takes a major step toward a positive personal outcome.

This Chapter is designed to provide an over view of the planned transition process and to identify roles and responsibilities of the principal participants (the new manager, the departing manager, and the gaining organization). It is designed to help ensure the success of the transition of the new leader and to prevent any unnecessary drop in productivity or increase in human costs. It likewise emphasizes the personal development opportunity inherent in the transition and provides worksheets to assist the new manager in the planning process.

THE CHALLENGES

Changes in key leadership positions within an organization are an accepted fact of organizational life. Managers are promoted, move to different geographical locations, or leave the organization and new managers are selected to assume their responsibilities. However, studies have shown that introducing a new manager into an existing group or organization results, in most cases, in a loss of productivity through diverted individual and organizational energy. The phenomenon is identified as "down time," "lag time," and "getting up to speed". But no matter what it's called, the personal and organizational results are mostly negative unless they are acknowledged, planned for, and dealt with consciously by the departing manager, the new manager, and the organization.

Figure 1. illustrates data derived from research in organizations with unmanaged transitions. As interpreted in this figure, a surge in productivity generally occurs when the outgoing manager's departure is announced. This is a result of the departing manager getting things cleaned up and projects accomplished prior to leaving. Then, with increasing proximity to the date of departure, performance drops.

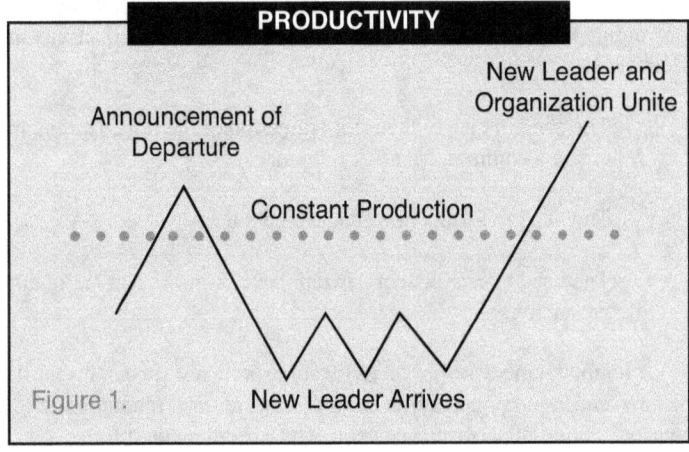

Figure 1.

PREVENT PRODUCTIVITY DECLINE

The announcement of a leader's departure and subsequent announcement of either a new leader or the initiation of the selection process may signal the beginning of a period of reduced organizational effectiveness and productivity. The announcement initiates change and a transition period that begins with an ending.

All endings create within us a sense of loss because it breaks the old patterns. In this case, the ending is of a certain style of leadership and management process. It is also a shift in relationship with authority which always stirs all who are involved. The ending will affect each person on the team differently as each begins to experience the loss. The manner in which the announcement is made and the climate of the organization at the time of the announcement will have an impact on the reaction each team member will have about the change. As people begin to deal with the loss, a period of organizational uncertainty and reduced productivity is created. This period or organizational uncertainty and reduced productivity often continues until a new leader is firmly established and accepted by the organization.

Without specific efforts designed to address the change, there can be productivity loss for an extended period. If the new leader arrives without accurate or complete knowledge of the priorities and procedures of the organization, additional productivity loss can occur. Although no two transitions are exactly alike, the following challenges describe the issues confronting the organization as it attempts to avoid lost productivity and effectiveness.

- The need to clarify the future direction of the organization and create a common frame of reference.

- The need to form a new management team.

- The need to establish organizational continuity and maintain productivity.

Attempts to increase productivity are usually not successful until the new leader and organization align themselves as a functioning, cohesive, and high performance team. The overall method for managing the leadership transition process effectively is described in detail in this Chapter. The process involved in managing the transition by way of this method is illustrated in Figure 2.

Transition Coach meets with new Manager to explain objectives of the process

1

- Establish rapport
- Answer questions
- Set tone of candor
- Outline process
- Review interview questions

Conduct interviews with new Manager and interviews / assessments with direct reports.

2

- Uncover key issues
- Promote openness
- Encourage willingness to deal with touchy issues

Conduct meeting, establish team objectives, deal with main issues facing the team, clarify superordinate goals and create personal action plans.

3

- Employ open dialogue as a method for dealing with challenges in the group
- Create support for the new manager
- Create an action plan for team development

Administer post-meeting assessment

4

- Review meeting results
- Create follow-up procedures
- Clarify coaching for team members

Provide ongoing coaching and team development.

5

FIGURE 2

PURPOSE OF TRANSITION PROCESS

The leadership transition process is designed to:

- Provide necessary information to the new manager and direct reports upon which to build a common understanding of the direction and priorities of the organization.

- Clarify expectations that the new manager has of the team members and what expectations the team members have of the new manager.

- Maintain productivity during the transition period.

The leadership transition process outlined in this Chapter provides the opportunity to significantly reduce the "down time" an organization may experience in getting both itself and the new manager "up to speed". The process provides the new manager with a methodology to acquire the information necessary to assume the role of key participant in the organization's decision-making process. This methodology also creates the opportunity for the new manager to learn. There is learning about important new people and learning about oneself in relation to each new person. The ***Dialogue™*** application plays a key role in gathering the intelligence that is the foundation for this learning.

CHARACTERISTICS

Several characteristics are essential to a successful leader transition process. If organizational effectiveness and productivity are to be maintained and even enhanced during the transition of leadership, there needs to be agreement between the new and departing manager that the transition process is:

- An integral part of the current job responsibility for both managers.

- Best approached as a process with distinct phases: Preparation, Transition, Evaluation.

- A team activity (subordinates, incumbent, new manager, superiors, customers, external and internal colleagues and Transition Coach).

- The responsibility of the incoming manager to initiate, and of the incumbent and organization to support.

- Tailored to the development of the new manager and the organization he or she is joining.

These characteristics indicate a time-phased program to maintain organizational performance at its highest level while introducing a key participant--a new manager--into the organization. The program requires the incumbent's time and energy to provide information so that the new leader can successfully understand the organization's purposes, priorities, constraints, strengths and weaknesses, roles, expectations, and major projects. It requires that senior management provide the new manager with an understanding of the context within which he or she will work, such as operating guidelines, purposes, priorities, and budget. The process asks the new manager to be open-minded in formulating a fair assessment of personal strengths and weaknesses he or she will bring to the gaining organization. The process implies full and open communications between all parties with a shared commitment to learning. Here too, the confidential interviews conducted by ***Dialogue™*** can play a crucial role.

A vast amount of information is generated during these activities and, if it is to be useful to the new manager as well as key members of the organization, some form of data collection, sorting, and analysis should be devised. There also needs to be skillful support for the learning and development process. The role of the Transition Coach becomes crucial in this regard. Time should be spent in the preparation phase making sure there is a solid relationship based on trust between the new manager and the Transition Coach.

FACTORS INVOLVED IN FAILED TRANSITIONS

When some managers take over a new job, things seem to go very well. They get along with their bosses and employees, learn the ropes, and after a certain length of time gain their own credibility and "own" the job. By contrast, other managers do not fare so well. Perhaps the single most salient difference between the successful and failed transition is the quality of the new manager's working relationships at the end of his or her three months.

Research findings suggest that in failed successions, incoming managers had poor working relationships with two or more of their key direct reports and with two or more colleagues, in addition to poor working relationships with superiors. Other factors which contribute to a failed transition are many including, interpersonal problems, rivalry issues, disagreement over goals, different beliefs about what comprises effective performance, and conflicts in management style.

The underlying common problem in most failed transitions is the incoming manager's inability to develop a set of shared expectations with his/her direct reports and superiors. Without common understanding, managers and employees are prevented from trusting each other. This is supported in research which indicates that developing effective working relationships is a critical task in the leader transition process. If manager do not explore important differences in expectations between themselves and other key organizational players in the very beginning of the transition process, problems will continue to crop up. This is the essence of the learning and development opportunity for the new manager.

Incoming managers who reported having major problems in the succession process point to conflicts in style with their bosses as a key problem. These conflicts arose partly because incoming managers had not clarified expectations with their bosses and because of less rational factors regarding what constitutes "good management." By carefully exploring style differences and related conflicts, both the new manager and the organization can learn the lessons needed for maintaining productivity. *Dialogue™* interviews with superiors cover all of these issues.

How can new managers deal with differences in style? In cases studied, the incoming managers had to take the initiative to work out differences and make accommodations needed for working effectively with their bosses. These are seen by many managers as soft factors that often fall into the "not for discussion" category and are, therefore, not seriously considered by the incoming manager in planning his or her transition. Only the most astute of incoming managers factor these issues in and give them the weight they deserve.

1 Issues Identification and Goal Clarification

2 Team Assessment and Development

3 Transition Meeting and Leadership Integration

4 Clarity on Superordinate Goals and Access to Coaching

Figure 3.

The Leadership Transition Process

Figure 3 illustrates the leadership transition process. It depicts four phases to be addressed during a planned transition. During phase one there are four activities that occur prior to the leader assuming his or her new position. The remaining phases take place at the time the individual assumes the position and within two to three months after the transition. The model shows the sequenced, interdependent nature of the key phases. Ideally, the phases follow the sequence depicted; however, scheduling demands may require the new manager to tailor sequencing to his or her peculiar characteristics and the practical demands of the organization.

THE FOUR KEY PHASES ARE:

I. ISSUE IDENTIFICATION AND GOAL CLARIFICATION

Figure 4. illustrates the four activities in Phase I of the transition process. These activities are building blocks that take place prior to the new leader's assumption of the position. They provide him or her with an information base for understanding the new organization--its purpose, mission challenges, roles, responsibilities, and "fit" with the environment. The understanding of the process and support by the organization are critical for success.

Activities Prior to Assumption of New Leadership Role

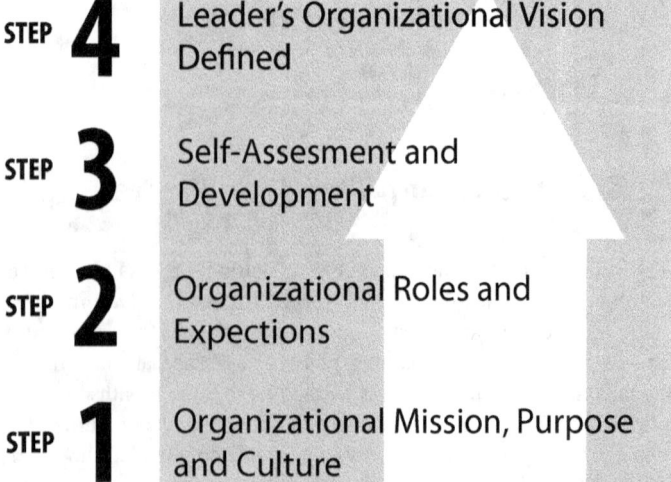

STEP 4 Leader's Organizational Vision Defined

STEP 3 Self-Assesment and Development

STEP 2 Organizational Roles and Expectations

STEP 1 Organizational Mission, Purpose and Culture

Figure 4.

A. UNDERSTANDING THE CULTURE/MISSION/ PURPOSE OF THE NEW ORGANIZATION:

A clear understanding of the culture, purpose, and mission(s) of the company that a new manager is entering is essential to his/her transition into that organization. The transition process provides an opportunity to become aware of the demands, pressures, and opportunities that the organization faces. The new manager should receive information from the incumbent and key members of the organization. Based on the understanding gained from this information, the new manager begins to develop a vision of what needs to happen in the future. Some of the ways the manager can obtain this understanding are:

- Review mission statements.
- Interview incumbent and other members of the organization. (*Dialogue™ does this.*)
- Interview customers. (*Dialogue™ does this.*)
- Review current management procedures.
- Discuss findings with superiors
- Study organization charts and reporting channels.

Some of the questions the manager can ask using Dialogue™ include:

1. What is the mission(s) of the organization? Are changes in the mission(s) anticipated?

2. What are the organization's
   - Goals?
   - Priorities?
   - Plans?
   - Programs?
   - Budgets?
   - Expectations?

3. What is the fit between present organizational mission(s) and future directions?

21

4. What are the key management principles and practices that are emphasized in this organization?

5. Who are the key customers of this organization and what are their demands?
(NOTE: "Customers" may be internal or external depending on the purpose and mission of the organization. "Customer" is defined as those organizations, functions, or individuals that depend upon the organization for services, support, or products.)

6. How well does the organization meet customer expectations?

7. At what does the organization excel?

8. How does the organization measure its performance?

B. ORGANIZATIONAL ROLES AND EXPECTATIONS

The initial determination of roles and expectations of the manager and staff should occur prior to the new manager entering the organization. This includes expectations held by key external senior managers as well as internal superiors and colleagues. The information provides the foundation for the development of the management team. This information, when combined with data obtained from self-assessment activities, provides the manager with insight into possible developmental actions which will facilitate his/her performance in the new position. From this data, the new manager begins to form a picture of the existing organization and how he/she can best enhance its performance.

The following are ways to obtain this data:

• Review job descriptions.

• Assess staff strengths and weaknesses.

• Interview key stakeholders (internal and external).

The incumbent can provide the new manager with job descriptions,

assessments of staff strengths and weaknesses, and identification of key stakeholders (internal and external).

Some of the questions the incoming manager can ask with Dialogue™ include:

1. How does the organization do business?

2. Who are my key direct reports and what are their responsibilities?

3. Who are the key stakeholders and what are their roles? What expectations do they have of my position?

4. What are my boss's expectations of me and my organization?

5. What is my boss's preferred management style? What is the boss's definition of good management?

6. What are the standards of performance and how are they measured?

C. SELF ASSESSMENT AND SELF DEVELOPMENT

Managers in transition need to make a conscious assessment of the strengths and weaknesses they bring to the organization. This knowledge is key to using the transition as a major opportunity for personal development.

There is no one point in time where a self-assessment is most appropriate. Good managers do this continually and as a matter of course. However, a formal assessment conducted with the aid of professionals allows the manager to more accurately identify those qualities that require additional development and/or modification. Once in receipt of this information, the new manager can continue to identify those elements of leadership and management most appropriate for his or her role in the gaining organization. The Transition Coach can play a key tole in conducting this self-assessment.

The following suggestions are ways of achieving greater self-awareness:

- Personal style, management /leadership values or personality inventories (e.g., Myers Briggs Type Indicator, the Kiersey Temperament Sorter and Career Anchors). You can take the Kiersey online at www.kiersey.com. By doing this before the Transition Meeting and having your direct reports do the same, there will be a common frame of reference to use in team-building efforts.

- Feedback from current superiors, colleagues and direct reports.

- Introspection both self-directed and with support

- Individual development plan

- Customer audit

- Management training opportunities

Some of the questions the new manager may ask him-or-herself/others:

1. What is my primary leadership/management style? How is it different from the incumbent's? What will be the impact on the organization?

2. What are my basic career values?

3. What are the strengths and weaknesses that I bring into the organization? How do they match the requirements and the team?

4. How skilled am I in building teams?

5. What means of communication will I be expected to use? What is my level of effectiveness as a communicator?

D. DEVELOPMENT OF AN INITIAL VISION AND AGENDA

The development of an initial vision and agenda for the organization is a natural tendency and a positive activity.

The vision gradually forms even while the new manager is still anticipating selection for the position. Once selected, large quantities of information begin to accumulate in his/her "vision database." This information can take many forms and can be generated both formally and informally. Some of that data is as follows:

- Articulation of how the new manager views the organization mission, goals, values, objectives, roles, constraints, opportunities, and priorities.
- Evaluation of information from the key stakeholders, both internal and external.
- Informal opinions from friends and colleagues.

This initial vision should not be "set in concrete"; rather it should be subject to modification and revision after the manager enters the organization and has had the benefit of more interaction.

As the actual transition time nears, the initial vision of the new manager begins to come into focus. After the departing manager has left, the new manager is free to actually merge his or her vision with that shared by the key organizational members. The successful accomplishment of this merger produces a "new" organization vision and agenda.

Some of the questions that are appropriate to ask during this "visioning" process are:

1. What are the overarching strategic goals and objectives? How do they impact on the organization?

2. What is the mission(s) of the organization?

3. How will they change in the next few years?

4. What are the organization's - Goals? - Priorities (formal and informal)? - Plans? - Programs? - Budgets? - How do they need to be changed, modified?

5. How does the organization do business now? How should it change?

6. What are the critical tasks that must be accomplished by this organization?

7. What are the specific organizational principles and practices that will help this organization execute the critical tasks?

8. How do I integrate my personal career values and goals with the demands of the new job?

After Assumption of Position

II. TEAM DEVELOPMENT

After the departing manager has left, the immediate need facing both the new manager and team members is the need for information:

- The new manager has already been collecting information. Further critical information the new manager needs concerning his or her direct reports includes learning about their roles, priorities, hopes, and concerns. How they relate to each other as a team is also important to understand.

- The new manager should also have a meeting with his or her new boss to get important issues out in the open. *Dialogue™* interviews the new boss and provides a basis for meeting and aligning expectations. Employees want to know about their new boss: his or her style, quirks, beginning vision, and agenda. They also want to know how they will fit into the new scheme, what the new rules of the game will be, and how priorities or their roles might change. *Dialogue™* enables direct reports to voice expectations and concerns.

The "Transition Meeting" is a key element in an overall strategy to develop the new management team and is designed to:

- Provide initial information for all at the same time that answers some of those needs described above.

- Set the beginning tone for how the team will operate.

- Establish the "transition agenda" or action plan for the first 60 to 90 days, while this new team begins to learn how to work together.

This transition meeting provides the foundation or backdrop against which vision, goals, changes, and problems are addressed. Some managers report that such a meeting has saved them up to six months of "downtime". It is during this process and subsequent meetings that  team members build confidence in themselves and each other and lay the groundwork for building the new management team into a cohesive, high performing organization.

Many methods can be employed in team building, but the new manager has the most complete transition database. Therefore, he or she is in the best position to determine what kind and how much of the following activities would be most appropriate to the organizational situation and circumstances. The Transition Coach can assist in determining what processes would be most helpful. The Summary Report from the *Dialogue™* interviews will be the source for designing the best agenda for the Transition meeting.

Activities such as the following suggest team building methods:

- One-on-one discussions

- Facilitated "Transition Meeting" Design

- Job descriptions

- Organizational charts

- Brainstorming sessions

- Physical challenge courses/exercises

Some of the questions the management team can answer using *Dialogue™* are:

1. What are the key business challenges facing the organization?

2. What are the critical tasks that need to be accomplished to meet those challenges?

3. What organizational principles and practices are essential to the achievement of the critical tasks?

4. How well are we living these principles and practices in the organization?

5. Are the people that work for us living these practices with each other and with their colleagues?

6 What are the key subordinates' current 60 to 90 day demands, priorities, and commitments?

7. How are decisions made in this organization? How should they be made?

8. How are organization and personal conflicts dealt with in this organization?

9. Who are the key colleagues that we must interface with in order to accomplish our objectives?

10. What are some things we could start, stop, and continue in order to improve our team effectiveness?

11. What are the new bosses personal objectives, priorities, major thrusts, and preferred management style?

III. NEW ORGANIZATION/VISION
(Articulating Vision, Goals and Agenda)

Having started the team development process by an initial clarification of the questions outlined above and established a working agenda, it is now time to articulate a vision for the organization under the new manager. This vision should be jointly developed by the management team.

It is well to remember that, in most cases, the organization existed prior to the new manager's arrival and will exist when the new manager leaves. Key organizational members had their own way of doing things and shared a vision of where they were headed, whether formally articulated or not.

If a traffic signal that said "PROCEED WITH CAUTION" existed for transitions, this would be the place to erect it. This is the time for careful reflection by the new manager and the organization. The assessment made prior to assuming the new position forms the "going in" manager vision. This, when coupled with the expertise and existing organization vision, forms the basis of a jointly shared direction for the future. Figure 5. shows the process of melding the new manager's vision with the current organization's in order to form the new organizational vision. As the vision becomes a shared experience, the organization begins to re-orient and change in order to accomplish the new vision. This process is accomplished by seeing the results of the *Dialogue™* interviews and the help of the Transition Coach to create the right Transisiton Meeting agenda. The outcome of the Transition Meeting is an action plan to implement the shared vision.

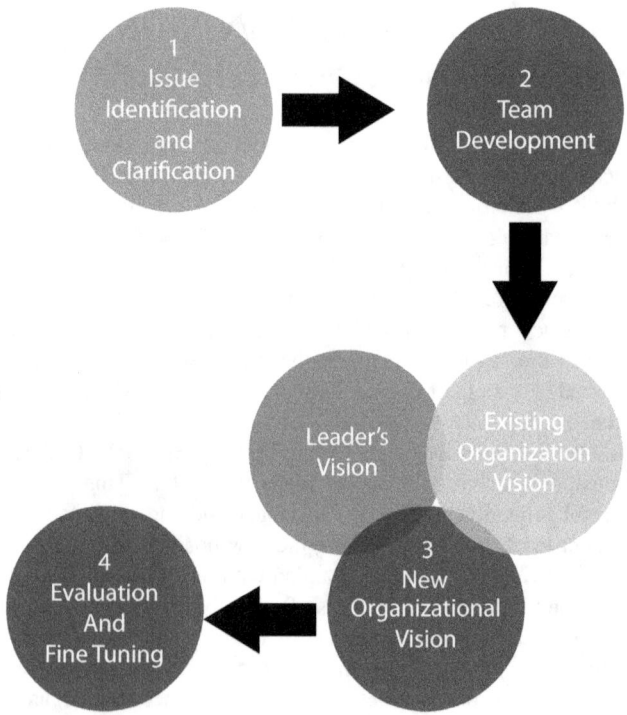

Figure 5.

Some more of the questions the new manager and the management team can address using *Dialogue™* are:

1. What are the key challenges facing this organization in the coming year and in the next three years?

2. What are some of the key events, developments, and trends that will impact on this organization in the next three years?

3. Who are our customers, and how well are we serving them?

4. Why does this organization exist? What is its mission?

5. How will the organization's mission change in the next few years?

6. What are our competitors doing?

7. What will this organization be doing three years from now?

- More of?

- Less of?

- Differently?

- The same?

8. What changes do we need to make in our behavior/style in order to achieve our future?

9. Are we staffed and resourced appropriately to accomplish the shared vision? If not, what can be done to get the necessary resources?

10. Are there gaps between my understanding of this organization's mission and where it is presently placing its resources?

IV. EVALUATION AND FINE TUNING

The feedback loop of the leader transition process is the development of continual organizational assessment. This assessment should include direct measures of leadership and team building activities, as well as measures of organizational productivity. The former measures provide an assessment to the extent to which the manager is successful in developing shared organizational goals and values. The latter provide  evidence regarding the success of the planned transition in terms of maintaining or enhancing organizational productivity.

The process can be a natural outgrowth of the team building activities as performance standards and role expectations are agreed to. This is a normal management activity that, if used optimally, can provide the new manager with a wealth of ongoing assessment information.

Additional methods of accomplishing organizational assessment are as follows:

- Organization surveys.

- Interviews with key customers.

- Interviews with colleagues and direct reports.

- Productivity measures.

Some of the on-going questions the management team may want to consider are:

1. What explicit agreements and commitments must be monitored, assessed and/or revised?

2. Where are the personnel shortages and weaknesses?

3. Have my boss's expectations of me or my organization changed?

4. Has the organization's relationship with key stakeholders changed? Should it change?

5. What are the specific commitments to follow-up and next steps?

MINIMIZING PERSONAL, FAMILY, AND ORGANIZATIONAL STRESS

An important, if often ignored, aspect of leader transition is the amount of stress it produces. Remedial action throughout the process can minimize the negative effects of personal and family stress on both the manager and his or her family. These actions are particularly important if the transition includes geographical relocation. Gaining organizations can and should provide essential support for this activity. The quality and level of this support may be particularly important for managers who have moved infrequently. If personal and family stress factors are not addressed, it may be difficult for the manager to focus on other aspects of the transition process.

Even less obvious and less often addressed is the stress endured by the organization during all phases of the transition. Stress begins with the announcement that a new leader has been named. Subsequently, any activities that promote knowledge of the new manager and lessen anxiety will reduce organizational stress. The transition process described in this chapter is a systematic effort to reduce organizational stress.

Self Assessment for the New Manager

1. What is my primary leadership/management style?

_____

_____

_____

_____

a. How is it different from the incumbent's? _____

_____

_____

_____

b. What will be the impact on the organization? _____

_____

_____

_____

2. How can I best assume the appropriate leadership style/role? _____

_____

_____

_____

_____

3. How can I build relationships that will support my new role? _____

_____

_____

_____

_____

4. What are the things I value deeply about myself, my work and my organization:

_____

_____

_____

_____

5. What are the strengths and weaknesses that I bring into the organization? _____

_____

_____

_____

a. How do they match the requirements and the team? _____

_____

_____

_____

6. How skilled am I in building teams? _____

_____

_____

_____

7. What means of communication will I be expected to use? _____

_____

_____

_____

a. What is my level of effectiveness as a communicator? _____

_____

_____

_____

8. What skills of mine are needed the most in this new role? _____

_____

_____

_____

9.
What habits of mine might interfere in my transition to this new role?

_____

_____

_____

_____

Organization Review For the New Manager

1. How does my organization do business?

_____ _____

_____ _____

_____ _____

_____

_____ _____

2. Who are my direct reports and what are their responsibilities?

_____ _____

_____ _____

_____ _____

_____ _____

3. Who are the key stakeholders and what are their roles? What expectations do they have of my position? _____

_____ _____

_____ _____

_____ _____

_____

4. What are my boss's expectations of me and my organization?

_____ _____

_____ _____

_____ _____

_____ _____

5. What is my boss's preferred management style?

_____ _____

_____ _____

_____ _____

_____

6. What is the boss's definition of good management?

_____ _____

_____ _____

_____ _____

_____ ____

7. What are the standards of performance and how are they measured?

_____ _____
_____ _____
_____ _____
_____ _____

8. What are the best times that you have had with your organization?
Looking at your entire expereince, recall a time when you felt most
alive, most involved, or most excited about your involvement. What
made it an exciting experience? Who was involved? Describe the event
in detail.

_____ _____
_____ _____
_____ _____
_____

Transition Review for the New Manager

1. What were the highlights of my leadership transition? _____
_____
_____
_____ _____
_____ _____
_____

2. What were the surprises for me during this transition? _____
_____
_____
_____ _____
_____ _____
_____

3. What worked well for me during this transition? _____
_____ _____
_____
_____ _____
_____ _____
_____

4. If I could replay my leadership transition, what would I do differently? _____
_____ _____
_____ _____
_____ _____
_____

5. What were the key learnings from my leadership transition experience? _____
_____ _____
_____ _____
_____ _____
_____

6. What specific leadership issues do I need to focus on now? _____
_____
___ _____

Chapter Two:
A Case Study of the Leadership Transition Program Provided by Leadership Transition Solutions

Executive Summary for Chapter Two

This chapter documents an actual leadership transition program provided to a major manufacturing company by Leadership Transition Solutions. The manager was assigned to a new role in a Center of Excellence set up to provide product and service support to customers on a nationwide basis.

Each of the procedures involved in the program are described in detail. The results are documented, including the evaluation of the program by the manager involved.

Introduction

The purpose of this case study is to describe in detail the Leadership Transition Program (LTP) as it is typically carried out in support of a manager assuming a new responsibility.

The study documents an actual Program carried out in support of a line manager in a major manufacturing company. The name of the manager and his organizational unit are disguised. John Adams is the name of the manager for the case study. John is in a Center of Excellence organization.

The LTP is designed to ensure the successful startup of a new manager. It identifies the key challenges facing the new manager and produces an effective action plan for the crucial first 90 days in the new position. Managers facing any new assignment need answers to the following questions:

- How do I prevent the loss in productivity that accompanies most leadership transitions and how do I move the team beyond a "wait and see" attitude?

- How do I get at the information I need about the organization, its strengths, weaknesses, main challenges and key expectations?

- What should be my first initiatives and main priorities?

Web-based Support for the New Manager

The Leadership Transition Program offered by **Leadership Transition Solutions** employs a combination of coaching support and **Dialogue™**, a web-based application that provides the new manager with the valuable information and guidance he/she needs to ensure early success. The process is described in the graphic below.

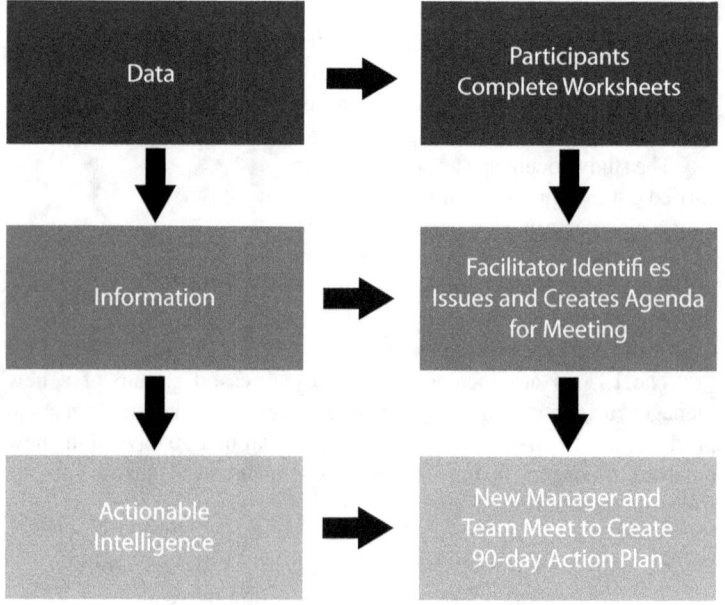

Application Worksheet Features

Dialogue™, The web-based application that supports the LTP assigns carefully designed Worksheets to all of the key individuals who surround a new manager. The Worksheets interview each of these individuals and capture the information needed by the new manager to quickly learn the real nature of the challenges involved in the new position. The key features of the Worksheets are:

- Distributed to Superiors, Peers, New Manager, Incumbent, Customers and Direct Reports.

- Promote honesty and assure anonymity for participants.

- Designed to be interactive

Program Participants

The graphic below illustrates the key participants in the
LTP surrounding a new manager.

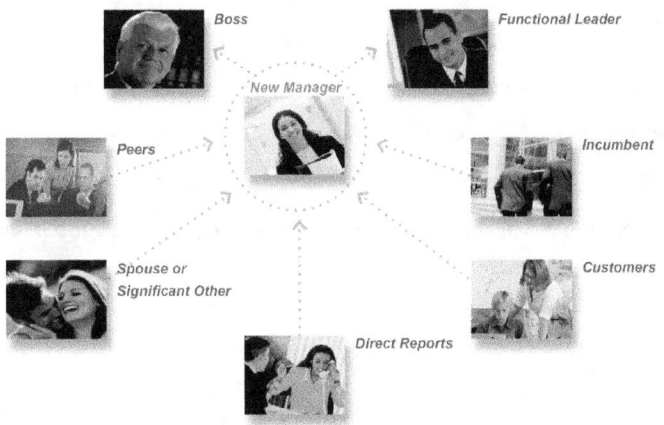

Boss

Functional Leader

New Manager

Peers

Incumbent

Spouse or
Significant Other

Customers

Direct Reports

Coaching Support

Once the Worksheets are completed by all
participants the LTP application creates
summary reports for each participant
category. Appendix A contains a sample of
Worksheet responses as they are presented in
summary reports. The reports are analyzed
by the Transition Coach to identify key
issues to be reviewed with the new manager.
The Transition Coach also suggests an
agenda to be used for a team meeting where
the key issues can be addressed and the
90-day action plan can be produced. The

Transition Coach acts as a coaching resource to the new manager and
is an invaluable aspect of the overall LTP. The Transition Coach also
assists the new manager by facilitating the team meeting that produces
the action plan.

Coaching Enhances the Learning Opportunity

Being informed about the issues and challenges within the organization based on the review of the Worksheet reports, the coach can be a real help to the new manger during the startup period. The transition moment in any organization is an almost unrivaled opportunity for learning.

The presence of a skilled coach during this time enhances the depth and breadth of the learning that can occur in the transition. In addition, the Leadership Transition Program becomes a cost-effective way of providing coaching support throughout an organization.

Case Study: The LTP for John Adams, New Manager in ABC Manufacturing Company (ABC)

John Adams was introduced to the LTP by Thomas Paine, a colleague who had personally experienced the LTP while assuming his new management role within the Human Resources function. The LTP was a positive experience as well as a real help to Thomas and he was therefore an enthusiastic champion about the Program and its benefits. The presence of this type of internal champion is crucial to the success of the LTP within any organization.

John Adams is new manager in a Center of Excellence organization within ABC that provides product technical

support. He has 12 direct reports whom he identified as participants in the LTP. In addition, he identified seven peers who are also part of the Center of Excellence organization to participate in the Program. He interacts daily with these peers and he considered their input to be of significant value to the success of his first 90 days.

Startup Procedures

Thomas Paine introduced John to William Pilder who oversees the LTP and acts as an external Transition Coach. Because of Thomas Paine's communication and enthusiasm about the LTP, John began his involvement with real commitment and willingness to invest time and effort. To launch the LTP, William made these requests of John:

- Send the names and email addresses of those he wanted to participate in the LTP and identify their roles in his organization, i.e., were they direct reports or peers. This information is needed to set up *Dialogue™,* the web-based application giving access to the Worksheets for each participant.

- Review the Worksheet questions sent to John by William and indicate whether he wanted to customize any of the Worksheets.

- Send a communication to all participants explaining the LTP and preparing them for the invitation from William to complete the Worksheets on the website. William provided John with a suggested communication to use for this purpose which John made his own and sent out via email.

- Set a date for when the Worksheets were to be completed by all participants.

Complementing Worksheets with Interviews

John did not identify his boss to be interviewed using the Worksheets typically assigned to the Boss via the website. Instead, he asked William to interview his Boss directly using Worksheet questions. A combination of Worksheet interviews via the website and direct interviews is often a good idea for an effective LTP. It is also possible to involve the incumbent leaving the position being assumed by the new manager when this is appropriate, but this was not the case for John's position.

Once William received the names and email addresses of the participants and the date for completion of the Worksheets, he was able to set up the website for John's LTP. As each participant was placed into the website database, they received an email inviting them into the Program with their User ID and Password for access to the Worksheets on the website. The deadline for completion of the Worksheets was two weeks following their receipt of the message with their User ID and Password.

Worksheets need not be completed in one session. Participants are provided with a Come Back Later button on the website so they can save their responses and have multiple sessions for completing any Worksheet. It takes about 30 to 40 minutes for completing a Worksheet. There are three Worksheet's assigned to Direct Reports and two Worksheets assigned to Peers. Two of the three Worksheets for Direct Reports are confidential and allow for complete candor in responses. One Worksheet allows for a personal communication with the new manager and is designed to help get to know his/her direct reports in a personal way.

Meeting the Deadline for Completion

The deadline for completing Worksheets was set for November 2, 2011. On October 31, William Pilder, the coach/Transition Coach, sent an email message to all those who had not yet competed their Worksheets reminding them of the deadline. Nine Direct Reports and three Peers met the deadline and John decided not to extend it since everyone had been given the reminder. John remarked to William that "Many of the guys stayed late to meet the deadline of their own accord, so let's move on."

Summary Reports and Analysis

William, the coach/Transition Coach, immediately began developing Summary Reports of all Worksheet responses. The application develops separate reports for each category of respondent, so there was a report for Direct Reports and one for Peers. After generating the reports, William read each carefully and highlighted what he judged to be critical responses for John's attention and for identifying the key challenges in the organization. The reports were sent to John in there entirety and included William's analysis. Appendix A contains a sample of responses from one of the Summary Reports generated for John Adams.

The analysis produced the following overall summary of the issues and challenges facing John Adams. It was introduced with this statement:

"This document presents all of the responses of the Direct Reports to the questions contained in the three Worksheets that were assigned to them: Dialog with Staff, Organization Review and Organization Vision. The first Worksheet identifies each respondent by name while responses on the other two are confidential. It is important that you read all of the responses on the first Worksheet, as you should know what each of your Direct Reports has to say to its questions. To save you time, I have highlighted those responses that I found most important. Certainly, if you have time, read everything so you can make your own judgments about what is significant. This analysis is based on my reading of the responses of your Direct Reports as well as those of your Peers."

Analysis

- Your team is struggling with overload and some confusion regarding roles. Two new processes are being implemented in the organization related to new product introductions and a new process for customer service. At the same time, team members need to maintain all the rest of their current procedures so the stress level is very high. Some immediate attention needs to be paid to this issue and some time devoted to overall team development.

- Role clarification for the team is an imperative.

- One individual on your team is creating tension and conflict with what was described as "Prima Donna behavior". This is the result of the individual being given a company hero award that has affected the team negatively. (William suggests a conversation about how to address this issue without alienating the individual in question.)

- There is uncertainty within your team about the vision driving the organization. The team has some clarity on short term vision, but there is no sense of a long-term vision for the organization. This calls for some careful work on the long term vision for the organization.

- Some team members are complaining that there is real resistance to needed changes on the part of more senior members who want to do things the way they have always been done.

- One of your peers has alerted you to a retention challenge with a very valuable member of your team. (William suggests a conversation about this issue also.)

- There is a need for you to lead your team in deciding what the immediate priorities are so they can "eat the elephant one bite at a time" rather than trying to take on too much at once.

- There is a substantial desire on the part of many of your team members to know more about you personally. One of the Worksheet questions allows Direct Reports to indicate specifically what they would like to know about John. (William suggests that John answer these questions as part of his team meeting.)

Using this analysis, William recommends the following agenda for a team meeting with John's Direct Reports. He arranges the date and time for the meeting with John so he can be present to act as Transition Coach.

Suggested Agenda for Team Meeting

Using Worksheet Responses from the Leadership Transition Website

1. Getting to Know Each Other Better as a Team (1 to 1.5 hours)

- Team members break into pairs. Each person in the dyad listens to the other introduce him/herself for ten minutes and takes notes for later use. Introductions should contain new information about that person, things the team does not know about them. After both members of each of the dyads has completed listening to the other's introduction, they then present that person to the entire group. This activity should be especially valuable for John who is new to the team and its new leader.

2. Response of New Manager to Worksheet Question: "What do you want to know about me?" (1 hour)

- John answers all questions posed to him/her by the Worksheets and invites discussion of his responses.

3. Getting Team Alignment on Vision (1.5 hours)

- Transition Coach presents all of the individual responses to the Worksheet questions related to vision and the lack of clarity related to long term vision. Then a group discussion is launched to develop consensus on both short and long term vision. Once consensus is reached John summarizes the vision articulation and indicates the commitments needed to achieve it.

Break for Lunch

4. Getting Team Alignment on Goals (1.5 hours)

- Transition Coach presents all of the individual responses to the Worksheet question, "What are the goals for the organization?" Each team member is asked to rank order the list. Then a group discussion is launched to develop consensus on rank ordering the list and securing alignment on each of the goals. Once consensus is reached John comments on the priorities that have been identified and suggests any additions or changes.

5. Creating the 90 – day Action Plan (1.5 hours)

• Based on the consensus developed in regard to both vision and goals, the Transition Coach leads the team and John in the development of a specific set of objectives to be accomplished in the next three months. Timelines and metrics will be created for each objective. A specific date will be set for the follow-up meeting in three months.

Evaluation

At the completion of the Program, William asked John to complete the following evaluation form. His responses can be seen to the right.

Leadership Transition Program (LTP) Evaluation

Your Name: John Adams
Program Start Date: October, 2011
End Date: November, 2005

	Exceeds Expectations	Meets Expectations	Needs Improvement	Failed
Ability of the Worksheet questions to capture important information	✔			
Usefulness of Summary Reports based on the Worksheet's responses		✔		
Support/ability of Program to help meet my startup objectives		✔		
Responsiveness of Program leader, W. Pilder (telephone, email)		✔		
Contribution of the Program to my first 90 days	✔			

What impact did this Program have on your ability to get off to an effective start in your new responsibility?

The entire process opened my eyes quickly to important issues that face me in my start up in the new responsibility. Especially important was being alerted to the role confusion issues within my new team.

Did the Program help you learn about the organization and its people more quickly than you would have without it?

Yes, without question. The Worksheets and their comprehensive compilation of personal and organizational information gave me crucial information quickly that might have taken me months to discover on my own.

Do you have any recommendations on how the Program experience could be more effective?

I believe providing more coaching and facilitation support along with the provision of valuable information and suggestions would make the program even more helpful. Having access to the coach of this Program over the first 90 days would also help me a lot.

Would you recommend this Program to others?

Please explain. I think this Program should be provided to every manager starting a new position within our company. This should include both new hires and those making internal changes.

Complete and send to: wpilder@leadershiptransitions.net

Leadership
Transitions Solutions

Conclusion

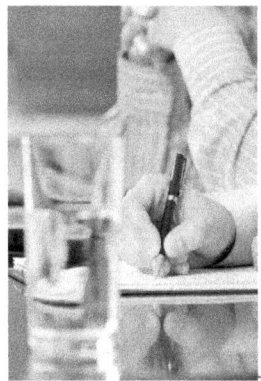

The Leadership Transition Program produced clear benefits for John Adams and his experience reflects the results for most individual managers facing the challenges of a new position. There are also distinct benefits for any organization that makes the Program a systemic part of their leadership development strategy. The following propositions effectively summarize the importance of the Program for any organization that is serious about the development of its leaders:

- The root causes of transition failure always lie in a pernicious interaction between the situation, with its opportunities and pitfalls, and the individual, with his or her strengths and vulnerabilities.

- There are systematic methods that leaders can employ to both lessen the likelihood of failure and reach the breakeven point faster.

- The overriding goal in a transition is to build momentum by creating virtuous cycles that build credibility and by avoiding getting caught in vicious cycles that damage credibility.

- Transitions are a crucible for leadership development and should be managed accordingly.

- Adoption of a standard framework for accelerating transitions can yield big returns for organizations.

From The First 90 Days by Michael Watkins
(Cambridge, MA: Harvard Business School Press, 2004)

Appendix A: A Sample of Worksheets Responses

Organization Review: Direct Reports

What is the mission(s) of the organization? Are changes in the mission(s) anticipated?

Anonymous

The mission of the FOE team is to provide a premium level of support to our customers. And within our mission parameters; to reduce the cost of external quality of our products. And to enhance the ownership experience for our "end users" or homeowners. With the change in minimum SEER ratings (10 to 13 SEER) and the future phase out of R22 to R410A; change within our industry is inevitable and should be expected.

Anonymous

The mission is to be the leader of the development process, to be the watch dog and try to solve problems before they happen.

Anonymous

To provide world class products and technical support to our customers. I feel the mission will basically remain the same but changes will take place to get us to world class and to maintain it once we arrive.

Anonymous

Corporate: Be the best in the eyes of our customers, employees and shareowners. FOE: Provide Technical Support to the field (tactical) Provide part availability support (tactical) Provide NPI Support as FOE Representative (project management) Provide technical training content Deliver technical training (tech/distributor conference,

Webex) Early Warning for field quality & reliability Catalyst for Escape Management process and Site Quality Leader Support Provide Service Bulletin content FSR/DSS Scorecard criteria Manage Concessions/EE (good stewards, proper documentation) Quality Kanban participation and Top Problem facilitation Product Change through E&T

Anonymous

Best said by our mission statement. "Our mission is to support the past, current, and future sale and service of RS products in ways that promote company growth through customer satisfaction."

Anonymous

customer support

Anonymous

To be the best to our customers and shareholders

Anonymous

Deliver a high quality product that is reliable and easy to install and service.

Anonymous

To achieve premier customer service. I think this has always been a goal but I don't think we have 10

What are the organization's goals?

Anonymous

We are driven by our customers. We recognize the importance of our people. We operate with Integrity. We strive for excellence. We deliver on our promises.

Anonymous

To improve product quality and reliability, and provide the field with the best support possible.

Anonymous

To improve the quality of our products. To reduce the number of customer complaints. To improve our information system and provide the FSR's and DSS's the necessary tools to handle questions from their dealers. To better train our FSR's and DSS's to handle customer issues.

Anonymous

DSS/FSR Direct Technical/Parts Support NPI Support Team Tech/Distributor Conference Support Concessions Process Management Warranty Analysis -Early Warning Quality Improvement/ Escape Support DSS/FSR Scorecard Management

Anonymous

Our goal is to support the FSR/DSS's with training, guidance, and consultation. In addition, we guide design, manufacturing with our expertise and knowledge.

Anonymous

customer support

Anonymous

There are goals in many areas of the organization from sales to quality to shareholder. The goals that impact our group the most seem to be 99% first year reliability and 95% 10 year reliability

Anonymous

Deliver what we promise. Exceed expectations.
Anonymous To add new procedures and streamline our current processes to maximize our output as well as quality of that output through NPI teams, new call routing procedures, etc...

What are the biggest challenges the organization is facing or will face in the near future?

Anonymous

The change in minimum SEER ratings (10 to 13 SEER) and the phase out of R22 to R410A.

Anonymous

The biggest challenge I see facing the organization will be trying to keep up with all the new product introductions that are proposed for the upcoming year.

Anonymous

Trying to maintain a proper level of customer support while trying to support the increasing number of NCI/NPI activities.

Anonymous

Maintaining the high level of quality that customers have come to expect.

Anonymous

The biggest challenge is to get engineering and manufacturing to accept FOE as having authority to stop product introductions if the NPI or NCI process has not been completed to our satisfaction. To keep the quality level where it needs to be.

Anonymous

Members of the team the older leadership refusing to use the process and remain in the crises management mode

Anonymous

With the advent of mandated higher efficiencies for our products on the horizon we must find new ways to differentiate ourselves from our competitors.

Anonymous

Dwindling expertise in the field Quality, responsible, accountable contractors

Anonymous

I feel that change as a whole is the biggest challenge right now. We are going through many transitions and it is sometimes difficult to get everyone going in the same direction.

Why is the organization facing or going to face these challenges?

Anonymous

Because the results of not facing these challenges would be unacceptable.

Anonymous

Because this seems to be new to most of us

Anonymous

It is necessary in order to improve our products, meet customer expectations, and gain market share.

Anonymous

While it is understood that competitive pricing drives cost initiatives it is important to remember that perceived quality is as valuable as real quality.

Anonymous

This is a drastic change from the past. Old habits are going to be hard to replace.

Anonymous

leadership refusing to use the process and remain in the crisis management mode.

Anonymous

Government regulations and an evolving industry

Anonymous

Competition is high in a basically unregulated non-self propagating industry

Anonymous

With restructuring always comes change and growing pains. I don't think it will be anything that was not already expected.

Chapter 3
Transition Meeting Design: A Manual for the New Manager and Transition Coaches

Executive Summary For Chapter Three

Chapter Three describes the Transition Meeting in depth and provides detailed suggestions for designing the agenda and activities for facilitating an effective meeting. While the chapter is a manual for Transition Coaches it will also be a worthwhile read for the newly appointed leader.

The Transition Meeting is a crucial event in any leadership transition process. It enables the newly appointed leader to bond effectively with the team of direct reports. It also provides an opportunity to address the key issues identified in the web-based interviews that precede the Transition Meeting. This chapter is a substantial resource for effective facilitation of the Meeting.

Transition events are also opportunities for building the culture of the organization and the chapter presents a set of principles and practices that can be valuable in this regard.

There are specific suggestions here for additional interviews to be conducted by the newly appointed leader or the individual who will facilitate the Transition Meeting that will complement and enrich the web-based interviews. All of the activities and agenda suggestions presented here are focused on enabling the new leader and the team of direct reports to produce an effective action plan for the first 100 days in the new assignment. The action plan will ensure a successful startup for the newly appointed leader and boost the productivity of the team of direct reports.

INTRODUCTION

Turnover in managerial or supervisory positions is a fact of life. When unmanaged, transitions can result in role ambiguity, reduction in openness of communication, and jockeying for position. Many employees report that during a transition period there is a tendency to turn inward and attend to one's own survival. When confronted with the unknown, unsettled feelings are created for the departing manager, the employees who remain, and the

new manager. Failure to recognize and deal with the complexities of a transition will lead to reduced performance.

THE SITUATION

The Departing Manager.

Once a change in managers is announced, organizational processes are set in motion. During this time, the departing manager begins to focus on things to be done before departure. Frequently, there is no time to be concerned with relationships that are changing or the future of the organization the manager is leaving. As a result, communications may be strained, and important decisions made too quickly or else delayed, until the new manager assumes authority. The closer a manager's departure, the more likely it is that he or she is preoccupied with personal concerns and thoughts of the next assignment. Ironically, the departing manager may have mixed feelings about how well he or she will be perceived by the new manager and how well he or she really wants the new manager to perform.

The Employees.

Throughout this period, employees may feel abandoned and anxious about what will happen to them as well as what will happen to the organization. They may feel awkward toward the departing manager knowing that the relationship is not what it used to be. In some cases, employees may feel relieved to be rid of an unwanted manager. In this situation, employees may create unrealistic expectations of what they want the new manager to be like. Whatever the situation, frustration builds regarding decision-making, and concerns about the future are heightened. As the departure day nears, employees tend to become increasingly cautious, anxious about the shift in power, and preoccupied with concerns for their own future.

The New Manager.

Taking hold of an organization is a period of intense action and learning for the new manager. If the new assignment is a big promotion or change, the newcomer may at times feel overwhelmed. As one new manager commented,

"You're on the edge of your seat all the time. It feels like you have no knowledge base whatsoever. You have to learn the business, the people, and the problems. You're trying like hell to learn about the organization and the people awfully fast and that's the trickiest thing. At first, you're afraid to do anything for fear of upsetting the apple cart. The problem is you have to keep the business running while you're learning about it."

During this period a manager is grappling with the nature of the new situation, trying to understand the tasks and the problems while assessing the organization and its requirements. Without knowing it, new managers are often insufficiently informed about substantive matters and find themselves making decisions slowly and laboriously. They focus on short-range issues and gear their efforts toward learning what must be done to supervise the most immediate and pressing operations. If the new manager's initial assessment of the organization is incorrect or incomplete, he or she may set the systems and programs of the organization moving in the wrong direction. The transition meeting works directly on these undesirable outcomes.

CONDITIONS CALLING FOR TRANSITION MEETING

The transition meeting is appropriate for all managerial changes. It is especially appropriate when the following conditions exist:

- A merger and/or acquisition.

- The new manager is unknown.

- Breaks in organizational continuity are dangerous and unacceptable.

- Little time is available for sorting and identifying problems.

- The new manager has a "reputation."

- The departing manager is a hard act to follow.

- Leadership style differences exist between the departing manager and new manager.

The following pages contain the basic concept of a transition meeting for new managers. Depending on the needs of the organization, the new manager, and the staff, there are a number of ways to structure the actual meeting. The transition meeting and its related activities are supported by the *Dialogue™* application described in the previous chapter. This application enables interviews and Worksheets to be completed online and the related data to be captured in a database. The *Dialogue™* reports are a crucial source of information for the new Manager.

TRANSITION MEETING OBJECTIVES

1. To provide a new manager with an introspective look at the organization's strengths and weaknesses.

2. To enable the new manager to get acquainted by clarifying expectations and concerns.

3. To clarify organizational priorities and key challenges.

4. To identify organizational issues that require attention.

5. To enable employees to gain an understanding of the new manager's preferred management style and organizational expectations.

6. To reinforce management practices and principles integral to building a culture.

7. To facilitate implementation of a new organizational direction.

MEETING PARTICIPANTS

The new manager and his or her direct reports.

TIME REQUIRED

Four hours to one and a half days.

Transition Meeting Design Flow

1. Transition Coach meets with new Manager to explain objectives of the process
- Establish rapport

- Answer questions

- Set tone candor

- Outline process

- Review interview questions

2. Conduct interviews with new Manager and interviews/assessments with direct reports.
- Uncover key issues

- Promote openness

- Encourage willingness to deal with touchy issues

3. Conduct meeting, establish team objectives, deal with main issues facing team, clarify superordinate goals and create personal action plans.

- Employ open dialogue as a method for dealing with challenges in the group

- Create support for new manager

- Create an action plan for team development

4. Administer post-meeting assessment.

- Review meeting results

- Create follow-up procedures

- Clarify coaching for team members

5. Provide ongoing coaching and team development.

STEPS

1. The new manager and a Transition Coach discuss the following items:

  a. Goals of meeting

  b. Time available

  c. Participants

  d. Meeting design

  e. Proposed interview questions

  f. Use of the *Dialogue™* application and its Worksheets

2. The new manager announces the meeting to participants (normally at a regularly scheduled staff meeting or in writing) and explains the purpose of the meeting. The new manager also asks participants to think about the items identified in the OBJECTIVES portion of this design document prior to the meeting. He also requests that participants engage in interaction with the *Dialogue™* application and complete the Worksheets assigned to them.

3. The Transition Coach coaches participants on how to complete the appropriate Worksheets on the Web site in preparation for the transition meeting. Tab F provides a schedule for interviewing participants directly. These face-to-face interviews are excellent complements to the use of the *Dialogue™* application and should be conducted whenever time permits.

4. The Transition Coach presents the new manager with the meeting agenda and modifies it as necessary based on the data collected in the Worksheets, the interviews and the new manager's preferences.

5. A proposed Agenda for a Transition Meeting and Transition Coach Notes are on the following pages:

PROPOSED AGENDA FOR A TRANSITION MEETING

TIME	EVENT	PERSON RESPONSIBLE
15 Minutes	1. Opening Remarks by New Manager • States objectives • Sets climate of candor • Explains his/her meeting expectations • Reviews agenda and role of Facilitator	New Manager
1 Hour	2. Bio-Sketch Start-Up Activity (See TAB A)	Facilitator

NOTES:

The Transition Coach introduces the activity by handing out copies of TAB A-p. 80. Participants write their answers to the questions. Seven to eight minutes are allowed to complete this activity. Participants then each begin sharing their responses with the group.

The Transition Coach writes down the expectations and concerns of the individual members of the group on a chart pad. These can be used at the end of the session for evaluation purposes.

VARIATION.

Participants interview each other using the questions as an interview guide. After they complete the interview, they introduce the person they interviewed to the group.

It is best for the new manager to go last in this activity. This provides the new manager an opportunity to hear all the other participants' responses and prevents them from mirroring what the new manager says.

Some managers may wish to address these questions at the end of the session (during event number 8). It is important that the questions be approved by the new manager before the meeting and be compatible with the specific work environment.

A word of caution.

The activity should not be rushed. It is important that people have sufficient time to respond to the questions and disclose information about themselves. This contributes to the development of trust among participants.

TIME	EVENT	PERSON RESPONSIBLE
1 Hr., 30 Min.	3. Each Direct Report in Turn (10 Minutes)... a. Reviews briefly, and informally, how his or her particular area of responsibility evolved to its current state, and comments on lessons learned. b. Lists his or her current 90-day priorities, commitments, and areas of emphasis. (The new manager provides observations at the end of the informal presentations.)	Facilitator/Direct Reports

NOTE:

Item a provides the new manager with background on the direct reports' areas of responsibility. If the new manager is promoted from within the organization, this part of the activity may be unnecessary.

Item b helps the new manager with his or her initial assessment. It can be included as a pre-work assignment. The number of commitments and priorities should be limited to 10. At the beginning of this activity, the Transition Coach announces that he or she wants the participants to rank their 90-day commitments in order of importance. Limiting the reporting time to ten minutes per participant prevents this activity from going on endlessly.

Item b variation: The participants are asked to construct 90-day commitment pie-charts. The charts can be divided into the priorities that consume the most time and energy. It is still important to give the participants time at the beginning of the activity to rank their commitments in order of importance.

TIME	EVENT	PERSON RESPONSIBLE
30 Minutes	4.Identification of the Key Challenges Facing the Organization	Facilitator

NOTES:

The Transition Coach asks the group to identify the key challenges facing the organization in the next six months (or an appropriate time frame to be determined by the new manager). The Participants answer this question: "What will the organization be up against in the next six months?"

The participants take about five minutes to jot down what they think the key challenges will be. Each person in turn reports one challenge, and writes it on a chart. This process keeps moving until all have identified their challenges.

The new manager is given the chance to ask questions about any challenge that he or she does not fully understand.

TIME	EVENT	PERSON RESPONSIBLE
30 Minutes	5. Organizational Priorities - The participants identify what they think the Top 5 priorities of the organization should be and provide their rationale (see TAB B). They evaluate the current status of these priorities and how well they believe they are executing them.	Facilitator

NOTES:

The Transition Coach asks the participants to list their top five organizational priorities using TAB B. Participants write down their priorities and include their rationale for selecting them.

Once they complete TAB B-p.81, the participants answer this: "How well is the organization executing the priorities (they have selected) at the present time?" The following codes can be used: (A) = Doing it well, (B) = Doing it, (C) = Not doing it well, and (D) = Not doing it. These codes are located on the right-hand margin of TAB B.

Each person needs to use the codes to present their list of priorities, the rationale behind them, and their opinion of the item's current status. At the completion of this activity, the new manager presents his or her list of priorities, rationale, and current status. These responses will be based on an initial assessment of the organization.

The advantage of this exercise is that it becomes clear whether there is alignment or misalignment between the direct reports and the new manager. Past experience shows that there is a high degree of alignment between the new manager and the direct reports. Seeing this creates a grounding effect for the team. A misalignment affords an opportunity for a productive exchange between the new manager and the team members.

TIME	EVENT	PERSON RESPONSIBLE
1 Hour	6. Relationship Between Key Challenges, Priorities, and Ideal Practices	Facilitator
	a. The direct reports review the 20 principles and practices or comparable company statement. (See TAB C- p. 82)	
	b. Select 2 or 3 practices that have the most impact on the attainment of key challenges and priorities.	
	c. The direct reports communicate the practices selected and their rationale.	
	d. The new manager provides observations on the management practices he or she wants to emphasize.	

NOTES:

This exercise is designed to get the new manager to: (1) identify and/or review key principles and practices, and (2) select the practices that are going to have the most impact on successfully achieving key organizational challenges.

In this exercise, ask the participants to identify and/or select the few key practices which will have the greatest impact on organizational mission and challenges. This activity serves to reinforce ideal practices and principles. The Transition Coach will probably not get unanimous agreement on the selected principles, so consensus building will be important.

TIME	EVENT	PERSON RESPONSIBLE
1 Hr., & 30 Min.	7.Clarifying Intra-Organizational Expectations a.The purpose is to clearly communicate the expectations of direct reports and the new manager in order to successfully meet the organization's challenges and priorities. b.Expectations are identified. (See TAB D) c.Individuals are given time to review and clarify expectations with other participants and the new manager in a series of one-onone 15-minute meetings.	Facilitator

NOTES:

One of the distinguishing elements of a team is its interdependencies. In other words, it is important that each team member feel confident relying on other participants to give them the necessary resources to achieve organizational goals and priorities.

At this point the Transition Coach hands out copies of TAB D-p.85. The participants write their requests using TAB D. A single participant will meet with another for approximately 15 minutes until each participant has met with everyone.

at the session. The duration of this exercise depends upon the number of participants.

TAB E-p.86 provides a one-on-one process for eight direct reports. It takes seven rounds for each direct report to pair up with all of the others. The names of the participants are written at the bottom of TAB E. The 15 minute time periods are posted in the time column. Location A can be one corner of the room and so on for B, C, and D. Post the completed copy of TAB E on the wall and start the one-on-ones. The participants will want to continue the discussions past the 15 minute period. At this point, it is important that the Transition Coach be assertive and keep the process moving on time. (Experience shows that the new manager is the worst time offender!)

The one-on-one design is not feasible with more than 10 participants. Most new managers who have completed this activity state that it was the most important of the meeting. It really pulls the team together and gives them the opportunity to express their true feelings in a relatively safe situation. As a result of this collaboration, group trust is reinforced. Participants lose their distance from each other, and there is a bonding effect between group members. This portion of the exercise is probably the most important. The participants will not be able to see the benefit and significance of this exercise until they have experienced it.

Variation

Each participant posts a sheet of chart paper behind his or her chair. Post-its are given to the participants and they write their requests on them. Participants need approximately 15 to 20 minutes to do this. The Transition Coach asks the participants to stick their post-its on the appropriate chart paper behind participants' chairs.

Once all the requests have been posted, the participants read them. Each person clarifies their list of requests with the entire team. As the participants are identified from each person's list, they have an opportunity to support the request, not support it (giving rationale), or research the request further before committing to it.

It is important that the Transition Coach keep this activity moving along. Initially, it will go rather slowly. Once people get the hang of it, the activity will move much faster. A side benefit of this activity is role clarification.

TIME	EVENT	PERSON RESPONSIBLE
45 Minutes	8. New Manager Comments on:	New Manager
	a. His or her initial personal objectives, priorities, and major plans.	
	b. The pressures he or she faces in this new assignment.	
	c. His or her preferred management style.	
	1. Under pressure.	
	2. When things are going well.	
	d. Communication	
	1. What kinds of information?	
	2. How often?	
	3. What level of detail?	
	4. What form will it take?	
	Both written and verbal?	
	e. The new manager discusses what he or she expects from the team in order to make a successful transition into the new manager's role.	
	f. Questions from interviews with direct reports (see guide at TAB F-p.87.)	

75

NOTES:

Normally, this part of the meeting is designed after the participants complete their interviews. This gives them an opportunity to find out a lot of information about the new manager. It also gives the new manager a platform from which to talk about his or her management style and initial agenda for the organization.

There should not be any surprises for the new manager during this session. It is important that the Transition Coach conduct the interview, collate the data, and give the new manager the results prior to the transition. This gives the new manager a chance to put some thought into what he or she wants to present to the group.

TIME	EVENT	PERSON RESPONSIBLE
15 Minutes	9. Closure a. Selection of issues to work on at a future meeting. b. Establishment of work groups to address specific issues. c. Evaluation of meeting and final obser vations.	New Manager

NOTES:

During the entire meeting, the new manager should make observations (or compile them) about the team. Before closure, the Transition Coach may want to spend a few minutes with the new manager going over his or her observations from the session in preparation for final remarks.

FOLLOW-UP

Within a day or two, the Transition Coach meets with the new manager to review the meeting and its results. Both process and content are discussed to ensure that the manager receives maximum benefit from the meeting. The discussion includes a review of action plans, commitments made by the manager, and any coaching on future managerial behavior that seems appropriate.

Approximately two weeks later, the TAB G-p.92 meeting assessment is given to all attendees. After compiling the participants' responses, the Transition Coach and the manager discuss the implications of the information. Results from the assessment provide a tool for measuring the utility of the meeting as well as a basis for the manager's future actions. In addition, TAB G provides a beneficial side effect by focusing attention on key processes during the transition period.

TRANSITION COACH CONSIDERATIONS

The following issues merit the New Manager's and the Transition Coach's special consideration:

1. The Timing of the Meeting. Experience shows that the meeting is most effective when conducted near the actual date of the managerial change. At this point, the new manager does not own any of the specific problems involved and has maximum flexibility in his or her schedule. The new manager's employees recognize these factors and feel relatively free to discuss issues in the hope of having an early impact on the manager. If the meeting cannot be conducted until after the new manager assumes the new position, he or she may have established a new method of operation and the employees may be unwilling to candidly address any problems. In other words, if the meeting is conducted more than 30 days after the management change, it becomes an evaluation of the new manager's behavior rather than a transition meeting.

2. The Length and Design Components of the Meeting. These components are extremely flexible. The minimum time for a productive meeting is about four hours. This allows time for introductory activities, identification of priorities and challenges, and the new manager's closing remarks. However, the optimal

77

length for most organizations is one to one and one-half days, which accommodates each of the suggested design components.

3. The Departing Manager's Level of Involvement. This matter must be carefully considered when designing and conducting the meeting. If the departing manager chooses to attend, he or she may find the meeting threatening and may be defensive when criticism of current operations arises. If the relationship between the direct reports and their departing manager is marginally good  or better, the direct reports may edit their comments to leave the manager with a good feeling. This may result in limited group openness and domination of the group by the departing manager. If the group has had previous experience with organizational development or effectiveness activities, however, the chances of this problem occurring are reduced. In case the departing manager does attend the meeting, the exercises can be managed so that he or she provides unique insights and helps to ensure that the group discusses key issues. If the departing manager participates, consider the transference of power to the new manager in all activities. Each manager's role should change during the course the meeting. Initially, the departing manager is active while the new manager listens, asks questions, and observes. As the meeting progresses, gradually reverse the roles. By the end of the meeting, the departing manager's role has ended and the new manager takes command of the team. In most sessions, the departing manager says a few words at the beginning of the meeting about his or her future hopes for the organization, significant accomplishments, and key lessons he or she wants to pass on to the new manager. The departing manager stays for lunch but does not return to the group in the afternoon.

4. Pressure on the New Manager. The new manager may feel significant pressure to make decisions about substantive issues. It is best to address this subject before the meeting and to advise him or her to defer any decisions except those that directly pertain to the transition. The participants need to receive similar advice. During the meeting, the Transition Coach may have to intervene to clarify the norms governing decision making.

RESULTS
A successful transition meeting:

- Provides a maximum amount of information to both the new manager and his or her staff and provides an opportunity to clarify concerns.

- Allows rapid inclusion of the new manager and bonding with direct reports.

- Sets the atmosphere for positive working relationships.

- Clarifies individual roles and expectations.

- Identifies issues for a future meeting.

- Reduces the time and effort expended by employees trying to figure out their new manager and vice-versa.

- Decreases employees' resistance to changes implemented by the new manager.

TAB A

BIO-SKETCH QUESTIONS FOR START-UP ACTIVITY

1. Briefly highlight previous educational background and key assignments that relate to your present position.

2. How would you describe your management style when things are going well?

3. How would you describe your management style under pressure/ when things are not going well?

4. What are kinds of things that can spoil a perfectly good day for you (things that irritate you, pull your chain, and trigger your hot buttons)?

5. What are the strengths you are going to contribute in this new situation?

6. What are your expectations and concerns for this transition meeting?

TAB B

ORGANIZATIONAL PRIORITIES

Please identify what you think the top five priorities of this organization should be and provide your rationale. What is the current status of these priorities? How well are we executing them? Use the four letters below right to state your evaluations.

A. Doing it well   B. Doing it   C. Not doing it well   D. Not doing it

PRIORITIES SHOULD BE	RATIONALE	CURRENT STATUS

TAB C

IDEAL MANAGEMENT PRINCIPLES AND PRACTICES

Below is a summary of 20 key management principles or practices representing an ideal. A specific company may have its own unique statement of such practices. Such a statement is helpful in the effort to build a specific culture.

ACHIEVING CORPORATE OBJECTIVES

1.
Makes clear the relationship between the group's efforts and the objectives of the Corporation.

2.
Involves subordinates in developing the group's objectives and establishing priorities.

3.
Ensures that subordinates are focused on objectives and are engaged in activities that facilitate the attainment of group objectives.

4.
Displays creativity in the budgeting process by questioning the relevance of even traditional activities and allocating funds appropriately.

LEADERSHIP

5. Sets high but achievable standards of performance for individuals and group.

6. Monitors individual performance and gives frequent and timely feedback.

7. Delegates responsibilities that match the interests and capabilities of subordinates.

8. Seeks advice from others and listens to it before reaching decisions which affect group activities and morale.

9. Appropriately shares decision-making power while accepting the full weight of responsibility when results are not achieved.

INTERACTIONS WITH UPPER MANAGEMENT

10. When discussing problems, provides upper management with suggested solutions and alternatives rather than simply presenting difficulties.

11. Gives upper management "the benefit of the doubt" by supporting necessary but unpopular decisions even when the reasons for the decisions are not completely clear.

12. Provides upper management with necessary feedback.

INTERACTIONS WITH COLLEAGUES

13. Makes sure that others whose support is critical clearly understand the group's goals.

14. Solicits feedback on individual and group performance from others.

15. Helps build productive relationships with other groups by constructively dealing with problems rather than denying their existence or blaming others.

INTERACTIONS OUTSIDE THE ORGANIZATION

16. Cultivates good professional relationships with relevant people in groups outside the company. 17.Identifies and evaluates environmental forces in planning. 18.Encourages active involvement in community affairs.

MANAGING CAREERS

19. Promotes development of subordinates through informal discussions and formal annual reviews.

20. Periodically evaluates the training and development needs of subordinates and provides needed learning opportunities.

TAB D
REQUEST FORM

TO: _____

FROM: _____

I want you to (clear statement of what you need)

_____

_____

_____

In order to help me (you fill in the why")

_____

_____

_____

I need this on\by_____

Receiver clarifies the request with the sender.
"As I understand it, in order for you to

_____

_____

_____

you want me to _____

on(date) _____.

We will check back on this on (date) _____

TAB E

ONE-ON-ONE PROCESS FOR EIGHT DIRECT RE-PORTS

1. New Manager_____   5._____

2. _____   6._____

3. _____   7._____

4. _____   8._____

ROUNDS	TIME	LOCATION			
		A	B	C	D
1		12	34	56	78
2		13	24	57	68
3		14	23	58	67
4		15	26	37	48
5		16	25	38	47
6		17	28	35	46
7		18	27	36	45

TAB F

TRANSITION COACH GUIDELINES FOR USE OF THE *DIALOGUE™* APPLICATION AND INTERVIEWS

Use of the Website and Its Worksheets

The new Manager and his/her direct reports should be encouraged to complete the *Dialogue™* interviews. It is essential that they complete the assigned Worksheets before the Transition Meeting is held. The Agenda for the Meeting should be directly influenced by the data collected with the Worksheets.

General Guidelines for Conducting Face-to-face Interviews

Start with general, open-ended questions

Review basic objectives

Let 'em talk!

Objectives:

- Obtain data on the needs of the team and uncover latent problems or issues from the past which ought to be dealt with in the meeting.

- "Plant seeds" for the coming meeting. Many of the questions can serve to encourage empathy for the needs and perspectives of other elements of the team as well as set a cooperative tone for the coming meeting.

Interview 1, The Supervisor

Some Sample Questions:
- It would be helpful to me for you to describe the new supervisor/manager's transition...

The opening question should be rather broad and somewhat

vaguely defined. If the Supervisor's answer is well thought out and structured, the Transition Coach can assume (and then test with further, more directed questions) that the Supervisor is truly orienting the new manager. If the answer is vague, the Transition Coach will probably have to turn the Supervisor's attention (by the way of questions) to each of the functions of  management and then discuss what his/her expectations of the new manager are in each area, e.g., "How much planning does the job require?" etc. The Transition Coach should also inquire as to whether these expectations have been clearly communicated to the new manager. Sometimes this discussion is the most useful of the exercise, and through it the Supervisor can begin to realize how many of his/her expectations have not been clearly communicated.

- What strengths does the new manager bring to this job?

This question gets the Supervisor thinking about the positive qualities/skills that the new manager possesses and enhances the chance that he/she will mention these during the meeting.

- What are the main challenges facing the new manager?

This or a related question usually encourages the Supervisor to analyze the transition from the perspective of the new manager.

- What changes are taking\likely to take place as a result of the transition?

Introducing "change" is useful; the Supervisor should be prepared to discuss the changes that are likely to occur--without this question he/she may be caught unprepared during the meeting.

- What actions are you planning to facilitate this transition?

If early questions have not moved the Supervisor to consider his/her responsibilities for ensuring a smooth transition, this question may. It also serves to "prime the pump" for possible action items in the coming meeting.

- What would you like to see the new manager doing in 4 to 6 months?

This question often encourages the Supervisor to consider once again his/her expectations of the new manager's performance.

- What does the new manager need to know from you?

Again, a question designed to encourage the Supervisor to consider the communication needs of the new manager.

Interview 2, The New Supervisor/Manager

- What were the main challenges of your old job?

This is a warm-up question. Since it deals with the past it is non-threatening, but it begins the process of analyzing job challenges.

- What are the main challenges of your new job?

Here the intent is to have the new manager compare old and new; to clarify similarities and differences and to look objectively at present problems.

- What new skills will you have to develop?

Teamwork will be enhanced if during the meeting the new manager can admit to the need for additional development in front of subordinates and Supervisor. Candor in the interview encourages candor in the meeting.
- What do you think are the main hopes of your direct reports? Main concerns?

Encourages the new manager to assume the perspective of the Reports and to empathize with their struggles in this difficult period.

• What do you need to know from your Direct reports/your Supervisor?

This question may trigger the expression of specific needs (which can be shared with the group later). At this point, it is a good opportunity to review the direct report interview questions with the new manager.
Option: Interview outgoing supervisor/manager.

• Ask question similar to those asked of Supervisor.

Understanding the predecessor's strategy and priorities is useful, not only for substantive reasons, but because such knowledge is likely to provide clues about current expectations and directions.

Interview 3, The Direct Reports (individually when possible)

• What are your expectations and concerns about the transition meeting?

• What unresolved issues do you hope to see settled soon?

• What do you think are the key challenges facing the new manager?

• What areas of the organization need the new manager's attention in the next ninety days? What is the new manager up against during the next year?

• If you could give the new manager one piece of advice during this transition period, what would you tell him or her?

• What do you need from the new manager to accomplish your

priorities?

- What do you need from your team members to accomplish your priorities?

- What do you want the new manager to know about the way things are accomplished in your group as compared to the organization she or he is coming from?

- What questions would you like to ask the new manager about his or her preferred management style?

- What actions are you going to take to make certain that the new manager's transition is successful?

This question prompts reports to see that they are active participants in the Transition and have responsibilities beyond "waiting to see if 'it' works out." Also prepares them to volunteer actions to help the new manager during the meeting.

The sample questions above normally set an open tone for meaningful exchange and can call forth cohesiveness and cooperation.

TAB G

POSTMEETING ASSESSMENT

For each of the following statements, circle the number that indicates the degree to which that statement is true for you. The higher the number, the more true the statement is for you.

1. I feel that the transition meeting accomplished its stated objectives.
   1   2   3   4   5

2. The meeting helped me to adjust to the new manager.
   1   2   3   4   5

3. I believe that I could have adjusted to the new manager as quickly without the meeting.
   1   2   3   4   5

4. The time I spent in the meeting was well spent.
   1   2   3   4   5

5. I believe that the others who attended the meeting wanted to be involved.
   1   2   3   4   5

6. During the meeting I discussed my real concerns about the change of managers.
   1   2   3   4   5

7. I believe that the others who attended the meeting discussed their real concerns.
   1   2   3   4   5

8. I believe that the new manager gained a better understanding of the organization as a result of the meeting.
   1   2   3   4   5

9. I believe that those who attended gained a better understanding of the new manager as a result of the meeting.
   1   2   3   4   5

10. I believe that a meeting of this type should be conducted for every change of managers.

    1   2   3   4   5

Complete each item below:

11. The most obvious result of the meeting was:

_____

_____

_____

12. The most valuable part of the meeting for me was:

_____

_____

_____

13. The least valuable part of the meeting for me was:

_____

_____

_____

14. If the meeting were to be conducted in this organization again, something that I think should be changed is:

_____

_____

_____

Chapter 4
Summary Report for an Actual Leadership Transition Program

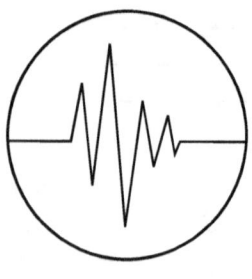

report for
Scott Johnson
Chief Financial Officer
Ajax Manufacturing Systems
Compiled by William F. Pilder, Ph.D. January 13, 2011

Executive Summary for Chapter Four

Chapter Four presents a complete summary report of interviews with superiors, peers, direct reports and customers conducted by the Dialogue™ application for a senior executive in a major manufacturing company. This individual was assuming the position of Chief Financial Officer (CFO) for a major division of the company. He was moving from being the Treasurer of the corporation to the CFO responsibility and facing responsibilities that were completely new to him. As a result, his transition was particularly challenging and the support of an effective transition program was essential.

A careful reading of this chapter will reveal the richness of properly conducted interviews with all of the key individuals surrounding the manager in transition. There is invaluable intelligence for this new CFO contained in the interview responses documented in this chapter. Keep in mind that the responses are those of actual participants in the transition of the senior executive described above with names disguised to protect confidentiality.

To: Scott Johnson
From: William Pilder
Date: January 12, 2011
Re: Observations on interview responses
The following responses from the interviews conducted for the Leadership Transition Program struck me as particularly important, so I have gathered them here to give you a kind of executive summary. However, reading all of the responses will pay dividends for you.

Responses from the Peers who participated:

Question: What is currently going on in the organization that I need to know?

"A lot of growing pains are currently being experienced. We are continuing to get better at the process "rigor" that has been established, but are by no means proficient at this point. If we are not careful, we will build walls between the organizations, and I have seen some of that recently. The biggest issues seem to exist with Engineering and Supply Chain. My take on the engineering challenge is an organization that is fearful of its leader, and fails to provide "early warning" of issues. The supply chain challenge hinges around organizational effectiveness and clearly defining roles and responsibilities of the new supply chain resources with those that previously existed."

Question: What would you like to know about me?

"I would like to know more about your "nuts and bolts" business experience. We will need your knowledge of processes and plants to make good business decisions and investments in the future. I

believe John worked hard to try and understand the plant needs, and it was very positive for him in terms of information flow, accuracies and commitment."

"Very smart and preferring to return to NJ one Night. Need to ensure you don't create the impression "you are passing through" regardless of your professional interests and needs."

Question: What pitfalls do I need to look out for? Or what potentially damaging missteps must I avoid making?

"Don't get so wrapped up in the functional actions of the organization that we miss steering the CS organization as a whole in the right direction. We also need to remind ourselves that the people made the organization what it is, and will help us take it to the next level. We also shouldn't "bow" to the pressures of corporate, but challenge "up" in the organization when necessary. I think it would be wise to show the team early, that you are truly capable of this "push-back", and not in the position to "only" carry out their requests."

Responses from Direct Reports

Suggestion: Read all of the responses to the two questions on vision in the Organization Vision Worksheet. I believe they suggest that you have an opportunity to clarify the vision that should be driving the Finance organization and create more alignment than currently exists.

Question: What changes do we need to make in order to achieve our future?

"I don't know what our future is. Nevertheless, I believe in the next ten years, this business will need to evolve to meet serious challenges pertaining to the effects and sources of global warming, cost of power, pollution and shifts in global power. This will mean we will need to evolve our financial capabilities to accommodate broader, more differentiated products, more product integration, different distribution and sourcing methods and an international product scope. Our financial systems will have to change and we need to get smart on how to do that. We will need to be more flexible, quicker and more efficient. We will need to move the application of our human resource away from data processing to analysis and advice."

Question: Are we staffed and resourced appropriately to accomplish the organization's mission?

"Yes and No. Yes; Generally people doing their jobs are adequate at what they are doing and have been in their positions a long time [Associates tend to know what they know and don't have interest or time to go beyond that]. No; There has recently been and continues to be an infusion of new personnel without adequate transitional planning and training by out going personnel. Little or no cross training or sharing of process/procedural expertise has occurred. Due to losses of capacity as well as capability, we are currently struggling with learning curves in order to accomplish the everyNight processing and analysis that our customers have come to expect as well as the recently added auditing/documentation compliance with Sox, leaving little or no ability to provide for real gain in productivity or process improvement (Deployment of Six Sigma tools; Development of new metrics and additional analytics). [No resource to direct and groom the forest for putting out all the fires on the individual trees] No; Lack of visibility and awareness to the processes of CS finance fit together and how what associates do effects the financial organization. There is no well defined and widely communicated career path in CS finance. [Don't realize that they don't know what they don't know]."

Organization Review: Peers

What is currently going on in the organization that I need to know?

Anonymous
New product introductions as a result of 13 SEER regulatory changes and ACCEs (AccuClean and CleanEffects air cleaners. Also have recently or will soon introduce several sourced products including boilers, humidifiers, energy recovery ventilators, and oil

furnaces. Need to understand the Ideal Home Environment strategy from inception through to current thinking, evolution of concept, product ideas, idea generation and potential impact to business. Need to understand relationship with Copeland and Lennox re: Alliance Joint Venture, exit strategies. Status of relationships with key suppliers -GE, Honeywell, TI, Emerson.

Anonymous

A lot of growing pains are currently being experienced. We are continuing to get better at the process "rigor" that has been established, but are by no means proficient at this point. If we are not careful, we will build walls between the organizations, and I have seen some of that recently. The biggest issues seem to exist with Engineering and Supply Chain. My take on the engineering challenge is an organization that is fearful of its leader, and fails to provide "early warning" of issues. The supply chain challenge hinges around organizational effectiveness and clearly defining roles and responsibilities of the new supply chain resources with those that previously existed.

Anonymous

Magnitude of change across all the functions and key drivers.

Anonymous

CCOE -recently termed financial leader; Vid, Ft Smith, Toledo, financial leaders all fairly new within the Co/CS. They will need/ want some of your time and will want to understand your functional priorities. Individuals are currently completing their annual reviews and goals. You should help ensure we stay on track with those that fall within the financial arena -directly or matrixed.

What recent key decisions affect me?

Anonymous

Unknown

Anonymous

The expected role that VP of Finance plays in the development of our strategies. The 2011 OP plan is truly a stretch, especially on the materials savings side.

Anonymous
Can not think of one (since you were already part of AOP)

Anonymous
Decision to hire another controller

Which key people should I meet?

Anonymous

IN addition to members of Leadership Team: Randy Smith (Ideal Home Environment) Louis Brown (AMS Sales) Jamie Jones (CS Sales) Paul Quisk (Parts Sales) Cyndi Port (ASWC)

Anonymous
Spend a lot of time early with Fred Frost and listen to the broad understanding he has for the business. I would also suggest a rather early visit to all of the manufacturing sites, and meet the people that make the strategies a reality. Randy Smith is a valuable "strategy" resource and very well organized.

Anonymous
Meet the NPI program managers, Site Finance and Supply Chain leaders, and Functional Finance leaders.

Anonymous
1:1 time with each of Dave's team; Bill Blart-Learning; Phil Brown-HR and filling in for a lot of stuff for me (Tom S); 1:1's with each financial leader and with *Sundi Cahill* (CCOE); Mina Smith-HR, and will help you with things like quarterly talent (HRP) reviews.

What gets rewarded in this organization? Individuals or teams?

Anonymous
Both. However, strong bias for recognition that goal accomplishment

is almost always a team effort. Teams are typically recognized and, if applicable, compensated from this perspective.

Anonymous

Typically teams. However, I am surprised at many of our "promotions". We have a great set of talent in the organization, but often gets overlooked.

Anonymous

Mostly teams. Still not very good at rewarding/highlighting individual accomplishments.

Anonymous

We reward doing the right work the right way. We have been shifting toward more individual accountability, but attempting to do so without compromising the current (strong) team dynamics. How do you like to work best with your peers?

Anonymous

Spirit of cooperation and mutual respect for the individual skills that can be brought to bear on goals/obstacles. Different perspectives and viewpoints should be voiced in order to ensure that the organization's best collective thinking is employed to tasks.

Anonymous

Open and REAL honest communications. I am one that tends to say the things that I believe the organization needs to hear, as opposed to what it wants to hear. I like that trait in people.

Anonymous

very open/candid and no hidden agendas. Face the brutal facts and find solutions in a win-win manner.

Anonymous

No surprises and open discussions

What do you want to know about me?

Anonymous

Level of familiarity with CS business. Where CS knowledge gaps

101

exist. What I can do to help fill in gaps. Perspective of CS and CS leadership at corporate.

Anonymous

I would like to know more about your "nuts and bolts" business experience. We will need your knowledge of processes and plants to make good business decisions and investments in the future. I believe John worked hard to try and understand the plant needs, and it was very positive for him in terms of information flow, accuracies and commitment.

Anonymous

Your operating mechanisms, aptitude for details, what information are you expecting from other functions and when.

Anonymous

Very smart and preferring to return to NJ one Night. Need to ensure you don't create the impression "you are passing through" regardless of your professional interests and needs.

What pitfalls do I need to look out for? Or what potentially damaging missteps must I avoid making?

Anonymous

Predecessor was well respected. However, do not mistake this for a lack of recognition of your skills. Perception of your ability and expected contribution is just as high.

Anonymous

Don't get so wrapped up in the functional actions of the organization that we miss steering the CS organization as a whole in the right direction. We also need to remind ourselves that the people made the organization what it is, and will help us take it to the next level. We also shouldn't "bow" to the pressures of corporate, but challenge "up" in the organization when necessary. I think it would be wise to show the team early, that you are truly capable of this "push-back", and not in the position to "only" carry out their requests.

Anonymous

Lot of legacy processes and practices work OK, but no one knows why they should be followed and what the consequences are if not followed. Refrain from making drastic changes unless you fully understand the original intent/boundary conditions.

Anonymous

Be careful to listen and understand first (obvious advice).
What should I be doing in the short term? In the medium term?

Anonymous

Learn as much as possible. Ask many questions. Don't be hesitant to voice opinion. Perspective is fresh, respected and welcome.

Anonymous

Short Term: Listen. Try to emulate the positive elements that Allen brought to the finance team. Understand your wide role, finance as well as strategy. Error on putting too much emphasis on strategy. Mid-Term: Challenge your organization to have more impact on the business, not just reporters of the numbers and audits. Have them press further into the organization and challenge at all levels.

Anonymous

Learn the business, processes (NPI/NCI), and organization alignment (who is responsible for what) in the short term. In the medium term, improve the finance processes/systems and operating mechanisms.

Anonymous

Meet the people (Dave's team, financial leaders, etc). Learn the business. Spend a lot of time with Dave. He will rely heavily on you and your organization.

Organization Vision: Peers

What are the key challenges facing this organization in the next three years?

Anonymous

Maintain sales growth of 12%. Introduction of IHE initiatives and products. Maintain/ re-establish position as technology and innovation leader. Successful launch of air cleaning products.

Anonymous
1. Six sigma maturity (i.e. really embracing and working under six sigma culture, particularly in operations)

2. Talent growth (mainly capability, some capacity)

3. Making IHE vision a reality.

Anonymous
Operationalizing the strategy; complacency and cost creep (headcount adds/nice to do's) -if the market declines...; low cost competitors; unknowns in the post 10 SEER market; retaining key talent while preparing successors.

Who are the customers of the finance function and how well are we serving them?

Anonymous
Leadership Team and direct reports to individuals on the team. Finance has functioned at a high level, but with expertise fairly centralized in the past.

Anonymous
All other x-functions are the customers. Finance function is serving pretty well, though improvement areas exist.

Anonymous
Fin customers: The CFO of AMS , CS, Dave Polk, individual business leaders, and direct reports (expectation of improving functional and leadership skills). We are much improved at providing actionable info. we are less mature talent mgt.

What changes do we need to make in order to achieve our future?

Anonymous

Opportunities for improvement include greater expertise and control at lower levels of finance community. Strength has always been ability to translate financial metrics and use to identify levers for achievement of financial objectives. Important to maintain this capability.

Anonymous

We must walk the talk in following the processes (six sigma, NPI, NCI etc). We must get clear around roles and responsibilities and execute well on those responsibilities. We must get world competitive in our base cost (both manufacturing and other base). We must execute/deliver on productivity goals.

Anonymous

Improve analytical skills and clarify local, versus functional needs. Ensure an appropriate balance between addressing local (site) needs and addressing functional or division-wide needs.

What are the biggest barriers to making needed changes?

Anonymous

Resources
.

Anonymous

Leadership focus, decisive actions, and a burning platform.

Anonymous

Competition for time is an issue as is the newness of many within the CS finance function.

What new capabilities need to be developed or acquired?

Anonymous

Honestly cannot think of any.

Anonymous
> We must get world-class talent across the board to add to the existing capability to become a great company ex: SQE, life cycle cost leaders, real product management, real quality and supply chain talent in our operations, required engineering talent in the areas of IHE/Electronics.

Anonymous
> Continue to improve the knowledge and application of six sigma processes. Who owns strategic planning?

Worksheet Responses from Direct Reports

Dialog with Staff

What are your current activities?

Don Night
> I report directly to Vice President-Engineering and Technology and Vice President-Quality as finance leader. I provide data gathering, manipulation, analysis and recommendation as well as controllership and accounting responsibilities. Employees served = 185, number of cost centers = 23, total base cost = $29.5MM.

Gary McKeil
> RS NDC Finance Planning and Analysis Team Leader (NDC Controller)

Gary Dash
> As Director of Finance for Marketing and Sales, I am responsible to ensure that the marketing and sales teams have the best possible financial support. This includes ensuring that sales and margins are completely understood on both an actual and forecast basis, that the expense levels are completely understood and communicated, that all marketing and sales promotions receive adequate financial scrutiny, competitive and industry analysis is done on a timely and

accurate manner, and that all corporate policies and procedures are followed.

Harold Lossen

Financial Reporting and analysis, Forecasting and Financial planning Operationalize AOP. Review and analyze promotional opportunities for external customers. Supervise administration of promotional activities for external customers. Deploy and analyze results of Six Sigma projects. Administration of incentive compensation plans. Ad hoc reporting and analysis. Develop and monitor business performance metrics. Maintain and monitor compliance with financial internal controls (SOX 404).

James O'Lirey

Within supply chain -productivity analysis, measurement, tracking, reporting, and reconciliation with finance Coordinating productivity resources/projects with sites, engineering leads, and supply chain Leading Six Sigma Black Belt project on the warranty process Complete finance activities for 609M budget (tracking, reconciling, accruing, etc.)

Jan Brown

For the past 3.5 years, I've been the CS Division Controller which had me responsible for general accounting, internal controls (including Sarbanes Oxley compliance), audits, FP&A, and warranty accounting and analysis, forecasting. With the recent hire of a new controller and Sarbanes Oxley leader, I will concentrate on FP&A, metrics and process improvements within the finance organization.

Ken Carnest

Member of the Toledo plant leadership, working with the team to develop the tactical and strategic direction for the facility. Normal daily finance and accounting functions for forecasting, internal controls, analysis. Developing team members to assume greater responsibility and enhance their individual skills.

Lou Ireland

Plant Controller for Houston Operations

Sundi Cahill

I lead the finance activities for the Compressor Center of Excellence

(CCOE). The CCOE is the only "plant" that has an income statement and balance sheet. In fact, I have 5 income statements and balance sheets each month, one being the Total CCOE (TCB). I have Reciprocating manufacturing in Dallas and in Houston, which is being outsourced. We currently have scroll operations in Dallas and Supieror, which is in transition to Dallas. Once the transition is complete, I will continue to have some salaried employees that will remain in Supieror. Some direct charges as well as cross charges will continue. I am also responsible for the financial reporting of the Alliance Joint Venture. In Mexico, payroll and timekeeping is under finance. My team must also complete financials for compliance with Mexican laws. We must report only our Mexico operation to Ideal Standard for Mexico reporting. Ideal Standard is a separate legal entity in Mexico and is reported as a part of B&K. As you can see, there are many situations in which I can only influence others to meet the expectations and deadlines but I have no control over their actions.

What is your professional background?

Don Night

My university training was in scientific/technical areas not applicable to finance. In 1q77 I completed GE's Financial Management Program and joined their Corporate Audit Staff. I participated in or ran audits for 19 business in the states and 9 foreign countries with aggregate revenues of $33B. In 1q81 I was placed in GE's Central Air Conditioning business as Mgr -Financial Planning. The business was bought by Trane in 3q82 and my job was to establish onsite accounting operations by 1/1/84. Managers, staff, office furniture, equipment, space, and software were acquired. Controls were established and documented and systems for general ledger, payroll, fixed assets, cash applications and accounts payable were implemented on time. AMS bought CS in 1Q84. In 2q84, I was moved to Mgr. -Operations Analysis and Accounting with responsibility for total business results, forecasts and plans. In 1q85 the responsibilities for Mgr. -Marketing and Sales Financial Support were added. In 1q95 AMS transitioned to a process organization and financial activities were moved into the process organizations. In 3q97, I was placed in my present position. I have been trained M+A evaluation. I do not hold an MBA or CPA.

Gary McKeil
> 20+ years in accounting -8+ with AMS -I've successfully started two
> companies (one light manufacturing -one wholesale distribution)

Gary Dash
> I have a broad background in almost all areas of finance with the
> exception of treasury and risk management. Areas in which I have
> worked and gained significant expertise in are: • Revenue Recognition
> – Assisted in the development of corporate policies surrounding
> recent stringent guide lines such as SAB 101 and SOP 97-2. My
> prior industry was software and project related and understanding
> the implications of these guidelines was essential. I made it a
> priority to work with our external auditors during the contracting
> phase of our major contracts to ensure there were no surprises
> with regard to when revenue could be taken. • Cost accounting – I
> started in a manufacturing company and spent several years in Cost.
> I have done and/or managed FIFO and LIFO revaluations, inter-
> company revaluations, obsolescence, physical inventories and the
> forecast of inventory levels. More recently I was responsible for the
> inventories in support of Ericsson's business with Cingular where
> I guided the improvement of inventory turns from under 6 to over
> 25 through the implementation of managerial controls. • Financial
> Planning and Analysis – I have held multiple roles in this area from
> the most junior role to being the BU manager for FP&A at Ericsson.
> I have significant background in budgeting, monthly and quarterly
> forecasts, productionforecasting, analysis of actuals, strategic
> planning, consolidations and eliminations of inter-company profit.
> • Accounts Receivable – I have managed the Accounts Receivable
> team for Ericsson in the United States. Accomplishments included
> elimination of all past due amounts over 90 Nights and driving the
> reconciliations of all inter-company amounts. As the Customer
> interface for the Cingular Wireless account I drove past dues
> from a high of 150 MUSD to zero. • General Accounting – As
> corporate controller, I managed two processing centers which
> we later trimmed down to 1. I implemented a process of detailed
> monthly reviews in order to clean up various issues we had such
> as unreconciled accounts and poor controls in the property, plant,
> and equipment areas. I also managed the interface with our external
> auditors. • Financial Management – I have managed groups as small
> as three to over 150 with 7 direct reports. Managerial positions that I

have held (all with Ericsson or GE) include Key Account Controller, Corporate Controller, Manager Financial Planning and Analysis, VP of Finance and Contract Management, Manager Financial Sales Support, Manager Strategic Pricing, Manager Bids and Proposals.

Harold Lossen

Several years with AMS as a financial manager with many years previous financial management for other manufacturing companies and experience in both public and internal audit.

James O'Lirey

I worked as a site capacity planner and group-level supply planner in a medical device industry. I coordinated lean mfg efforts, developed scheduling models, cycle time targets, kanban levels, WIP amounts, raw material/inventory levels, etc. in order to achieve highest fill rate for finishing plants. In my second job, I trained in six sigma and completed several process improvement projects in a service industry.

Jan Brown

I've been with AMS for over 20 years with 2 years in Engineering, 7 years in Marketing and the remainder in finance. I've had a wide variety of assignments including leading two operations (Payroll for 4 years and Extended Warranty for 7 years) and most recently, Division Controller. My college education is in mathematics (BS in theoretical, MS in applied) but I'm also a graduate of General Electric's Financial Management Program and Confidential Systems Leadership Program.

Ken Carnest

General Electric Appliances group, general accounting, capital through plant manufacturing for Range division. General Electric/ Lockheed Martin Aerospace. Green field plant start-up with GE through sale and plant closure due to restructuring by Lockheed Martin. Implementation, MRP, shop floor quality and labor tracking systems. Hiring hourly workforce. Shifted to Operations & IS role after initial finance systems and process were in place. Allied Signal -Site controller Pittsburg Kansas -Responsible for IS, Purchasing,

Stores, and logistics. Allied Signal -Site Controller PhiladelphiaPA Same responsibilities (excluding logistics) in a larger facility. CPM certification. Sunoco -Mfg Finance manager for acquired Aristech sites including former Allied Signal Philadelphia facility sold to Sunoco (HQ role) All plant manufacturing costs. Focus on restructuring the group, consolidating back room operations, more emphasis on analysis versus reporting the past. These sites had payroll, A/P all cost analysis and inventory.

Lou Ireland

Graduated Magna Cum Laude with a BS in Finance from Boston College. Graduated from the General Electric Financial Management Program. Spent 10 years with GE in Pittsfield, Mass in various assignments -Accts Pay, Gen'l Acct'g, Billing, Mfg Acct'g, Cost Est., Group Acct'g. Transferred to Lynchburg Va. in 1978 and held positions in Group Acct'g and International Analysis. Transferred to Ft. Smith in 1981 as Plant Controller. Transferred to Houston Tx in 1984 as Mgr of Gen'l Acct'g -included Payroll, AP, and Gen'l Acct'g. Transferred to current position in 1987 -at the time it included responsibilities for the Toledo Plant as well. Participated in the Second "Leadership UPG" Class in 1999. Have participated on many special projects including the justification of moving heaters from Mexico to the Springhill facility and numerous compressor studies, including working on JV studies with Daiken and Sanyo, attempting to purchase Maneurop, and the study that ended with the initial JV with Lennox Int'l.

Sundi Cahill

I have a BBA from The University of Texas at Austin and an ABA from Houston Junior College. While completing my degree, I worked for a CPA firm in Austin. Since being in Houston, I have also continued my learning with a Cost Accounting class from The University of Texas at Houston (2000). Upon relocating to Houston in 1995, I joined Trane in Finance working for the CS CFO. Within the year, I moved into Personnel Accounting as the Benefits Specialist. In 1998 (the year we built the compressor plant in Mexico), I joined the Compressor Group as a Base Cost Accountant. I have held a number of positions with increasing responsibility for the Compressor Group including Cost Accounting, Houston Finance Leader, Compressor Group Controller and currently Controller for the CCOE.

Briefly describe yourself in terms of what you would like for me to know about you personally.

Don Night

I'm married with three college age sons. I have numerous avocations which occupy my spare time.

Gary McKeil

Like to play golf, go boating, fishing

Gary Dash

I am fiercely loyal and ethical. I am diligent to my task and take great pride that my team does the best possible. I live up to my commitments and expect the same from my staff. I also like to have fun at work.

Harold Lossen

I am a dedicated, energetic and knowledgeable financial professional with a solid history of accomplishments with increasing levels of leadership responsibilities.

James O'Lirey

I'm originally from New Jersey. I completed my degree in Industrial Engineering from Georgia Tech (and am currently back in school part time for my MBA) Besides the above, I've also lived in Arizona and West Texas for a little while. I'm a huge Denver Broncos fan (go to Denver once a year to watch them play). I like to keep a positive attitude -especially at work -and always try to keep things in perspective (which is hard in the finance organization sometimes!!)

Jan Brown

I'm a very dedicated and hard working employee but when I do go home, I love to Brown and work in my yard.

Ken Carnest

Solid background in manufacturing, appliances, aerospace, bulk and specialty chemicals. I have sought and taken cross functional roles in operations and IS to gain experience not otherwise available. Really do enjoy developing people and seeing them succeed.

Lou Ireland

Very serious about the financial responsibilities assigned to us. Completing the responsibilities of the position in a professional manner is very important to me. Would be interested in a Group OF Finance position, if one ever opens. I also have a personal life, which includes a wife of almost 37 years, two children, and a grandson. I enjoy playing golf -or more accurately stated -spending time on the golf course. I enjoy yard work, reading, and most sports.

Sundi Cahill

I have a wonderful husband, Kyle, daughter, Kelli (7) and son, Koen (4). I am very active in my Church. As for work, I want to be challenged and I enjoy what I am doing. I would like to learn skills that would lead to a larger responsibility in CS or another AMS business while advancing my career. I am a Six Sigma Certified Green Belt. My short term goal is the CCOE Finance Leader position, created in February and vacated in November.

What do you see are the strengths of the organization?

Don Night

CS Finance is the most efficient and effective organization of its kind in AMS. Our analytical expertise has been unrivaled. An intensity, adaptability and willingness to work hard that are hallmarks within CS.

Gary McKeil

Its people -their dedication, creativity, and expertise

Gary Dash

We have some extremely knowledgeable people who know a great deal about the business and all of the processes. In my area that is also a weakness in that we are loosing that expertise through retirement and illness. That expertise has to be rebuilt.

Harold Lossen

Historically, AMS Systems has enjoyed a stable position within an expanding marketplace while retaining a wealth of personnel with long tenures and industry leading technical expertise. Financial organization has also held personnel with a wealth of business knowledge related to systems and procedures. (People and their dedication)

James O'Lirey
Diligence, perseverance, going above and beyond, doing things because they're right, dedication

Jan Brown
We have many very experienced, hard working and dedicated individuals in the finance function.

Ken Carnest
Some good long service core knowledge in the finance group and a great work ethic.Some new people in the mix bringing new perspecitves and experiences to the team.

Lou Ireland
My Team has a lot of experience and performs their tasks very professionally. The Finance Organization itself has always looked for the smartest ways of completing our responsibilities -which involves a lot of computer spreadsheets and systems, and a minimum of manual intervention. Very efficient group of individuals.

Sundi Cahill
The Finance organization excels in execution. Give us a situation and we can solve it. SOX is an example of our execution. Jan's direction and leadership is very much a part of our strength. Each of the Finance Leaders take pride in our own area or plant.

What are your ideas about things that we should stop doing?

Don Night
The way we do SARBOX should be reviewed particularly in comparison with other companies, perhaps using a consultant.

The purpose would be improving the efficiency with which we do SARBOX compliance and implementing 21st century routines and controls consistent with the changing business needs.

Gary McKeil

Fewer audits (or consolidate them); fewer redundant questions for the same information for the same period of time from multiple people; get a handle on the out-of-control email requests

Gary Dash

It appears to me that we go into too much detail on monthly financial forecasts. Quarterly detailed forecasts with monthly updates on sales and margins per the latest production updates would seem to be more efficient.

Harold Lossen

Stop heavy reliance on people rather than systems and processes.

James O'Lirey

I think we do a good job for the most part (e.g. we have standing meetings, but we actually talk about worthwhile stuff in them!)

Jan Brown

I think we've done a good job of taking out non-value added activity over the past few years since we had to concentrate so much time on Sarbanes-Oxley. That being said, I think we should evaluate some of our Sarbox activities to determine if we have overall monitoring controls that may take the place of some of the low level, tedious and non-value added controls put in place.

Ken Carnest

Stopping the 6 Sigma tracking is a great example. Eliminate redundant reporting and driving people to call things 6 Sigma because they felt they had to. Let people explain why a productivity measure might be skewed in their reviews vs letting people open the windows to eliminating data that does not reflect well on their particular measure.

Lou Ireland

We need to get smarter with our Sarbanes Oxley auditing -the entire Company, not just us. We spend too much time completing the audits and it is very resource intensive. It is not well understood that this is not just a "Finance Thing". We also need to get E&Y to look at areas other than just Houston. We have been spending a great deal of time during the last two years with auditors, at the expense of some of our other responsibilities.

Sundi Cahill

Duplicate work. Some things that should be routine are completed differently by each plant. We desperately need to standardize. I have found this first hand as I have had to create the CCEO finance department. In providing training for new employees, I have found that we do not share best practices very well. We should also stop working "around" systems and make the systems work for us. There are countless reports or processes that have been developed or are in place because a "system" can't do something for us so we must adjust. Eliminate non-value added work so we can work "on" the business instead of "in" the business.

What are your ideas about things that we should start doing?

Don Night

Short-term -Get the business processes synched up to generate high levels of productivity on a realized basis. Long-term -Work with IT to establish a migration plan for financial systems which can use the best of mainframe and client/server technology so that, with new software, finance can maintain or enhance its service and efficiency. Also get CS Finance prepared to serve a product/customer matrix dealing with 21st century issues like global warming, high power cost, pollution.

Gary McKeil

Allow time for the Controllers to focus on the needs & productivity improvements at their respective sites

Gary Dash

I have seen a couple of things that I have found troubling. Accepting data without understanding it or checking it for reasonableness is something I am going to strive to change in the coming year. I also do not think that we provide enough information.

We are great in supplying details, but I want the team to focus on providing the level of analysis that saves the reader time instead of forcing him/her to analyze it themselves to determine what the details provide.

Harold Lossen

Upgrade or replace current processes with documented and stable processes in place with integrated cross training of finance personnel.

James O'Lirey

We had a group meeting last year for a few nights in Dallas and I think that was a very successful endeavor. We talked about doing it once or twice a year in a different location each time, but haven't heard anything about that. I think that finance is in an interesting situation since we're a supporting group for our respective entities, but there isn't a tremendous amount of finance cohesion and being offsite together helped a lot.

Jan Brown

I believe we should use our weekly finance meetings to allow others to share / present best practices.

Ken Carnest

Consistency in measuring productivity. Look at where our staff resources are and should some back room tasks be consolidated further in a particular site or HQ location. This does not necessarily mean a headcount cut at a site if we can focus more on analysis and less on transactional and at the same time help the operations run more effectively.

Lou Ireland

Determine why we find it necessary to go outside for talent. We have HRP's, PMP's, PDP's, Leadership Classes, etc., yet we find it necessary to go outside to fill key positions. This is not just a "Finance Thing".

Sundi Cahill

We should have two Finance Leader meetings (at different sites) annually. We had one earlier this year in the Dallas plant and feedback indicated it was very successful (we are ready to host another one) and a desire to want more. Not only from the learning and information sharing that took place, but also from a "getting to know you" standpoint. We have so many new faces in Finance and it really helped me to put a face with a name and spend some time getting to know the newer members of the team. Share best practices and automate standard requirements across CS finance. SOX has created the need to focus in this area. There are best practices that come out of auditing each other's plant that would be very nice to capitalize on but it is just not a group priority. In most cases, time is the one thing that prevents us from doing it ourselves. One other area we should focus on is systems. There are real examples of low hanging fruit that could improve productivity if we just had some focused systems expertise to bridge the finance knowledge with the system capabilities. Six Sigma tools should also be utilized to help us with productivity. I view this as a temporary assignment (or consultant work) that would more than pay for itself.

Are there any promises or commitments made to you that I should know?

Don Night
None

Gary McKeil
None

Gary Dash
None

Harold Lossen
A promotion was committed and communicated almost two months ago but has not been fulfilled.

James O'Lirey
Yes, still waiting for my private jet.... (just kidding)

Jan Brown
When splitting my job into two (Controller and FP&A leader), Allen said that my job would be the bigger of the two roles. I'm sure we will talk about this in the next few weeks.

Ken Carnest
> None......

Lou Ireland
> No.

Sundi Cahill
> No, except for further development in strategic financial skills.

What do you want to know about me?

Don Night
> Your predecessor's strength was upward communication. What can
> we do to help you maintain that capability? What are your goals for
> the Finance organization? What are your personal goals for the time
> you're in CS Finance? Your predecessor was not interested in CS
> Finance. Anything you are able to do to improve on that history will
> be very positive.

Gary McKeil
> Will you respond to legitimate concerns/needs -if not, that is OK; it
> just helps to know.

Gary Dash
> I would like to understand your management style and a bit more of
> your background.

Harold Lossen
> What is your assessment of the immediate need of the organization?
> What is your view of finance's role within the CS organization?
> What can you do to facilitate the transfer of our business vision into
> a measurable and actionable financial process roadmap?

James O'Lirey
> Personal background, history, work philosophy, what drive you,
> what goals do you have

Jan Brown
> What is your vision for CS Finance?

Ken Carnest

Not at this time. We had our brief meeting. Lou Ireland What attracted you to the CS Finance position and what do you believe it was that you

had done in the past that prepared you for the position (Related to 6 above).

Sundi Cahill

What is your vision for CCOE Finance? What are your talent development plans to build functional excellence across CS.

Is there anything specific that you want me to do?

Don Night

1. Take full advantage of *Jan Brown*'s capabilities without overwhelming her.
2. Work to expand Finance's product offering not only to the Leadership team but also to the other tiers.
3. The forecasting process for sales, production and inventory is "broken" and must be fixed. In a good year like '05, it's doesn't hurt too badly but in a tougher year such as '06 may be, the pain can be serious particularly with the productivity targets we have.

Gary McKeil

Talk with Fred Frost and the two of you make a final determination as to whether we can add a head or partial head (and when) to the NDC Finance team to focus on Cincom. (I would prefer Finance work stay in the Finance area) -Then communicate that final decision to me.

Gary Dash

I would like to be kept as informed as possible of anything that could influence how I do my job. I should do the same in return.

Harold Lossen

Communicate as specifically and as timely as possible expectations Provide feedback frequently -celebrate achievements / analyze shortfalls Provided needed resources Remove barriers to success

James O'Lirey

I think the finance organization is really strong, but in general, there seems to be a morale problem (esp as opposed to Supply Chain, etc.) If you could do things to boost finance morale then I would consider it a success!

Jan Brown

Communicate, communicate, communicate.

Ken Carnest

I felt comfortable after our conversation with the idea I can e-mail or call you with an issue, but nothing at the moment.

Lou Ireland

Just give your support......

Sundi Cahill

Learn the many complexities in the CCOE that do not exist in other plants and other areas. Assistance in driving change when necessary, or to achieve productivity. We are the only CCOE that spans two businesses (AMS and CS), we are the only CCOE that operates in multiple locations and multiple countries with systems designed to operating in one location and we are in a constant state of change. I am hopeful that you will continue to support the CCOE, when I am pushed to conform to "systems or policies" that require additional work to bridge the gap. An example is the monthly exercise to move the Supieror Scroll production from AMS to CS each month end. The CCOE is required to meet the same deadline but we do not get our information in a timely manner (because of different deadlines from TCS) which appears to be a consistent lack of performance on our part. Please (because of lack of common Trane systems) is made in order to achieve things that for others is routine and somewhat simple. Expose me to senior CS and AMS leadership so that I can become more prepared to give financial guidance and present ideas that drive the business.

Organization Review: Direct Reports

What are the biggest challenges the organization is facing or will face in the near future?

121

Anonymous

Short term issues include turnover, sales and production forecasting, cash flow forecasting, productivity implementation. Other challenges include building an organization structure which helps provide internal growth and the assurance of a strong up and coming bench to cover retirements.

Anonymous

Obtaining $400MM in segment income in 2010; manufacturing capacity issues vs warehousing more inventory; continuing to be a dominant leader in HVAC while the Asians start to make inroads into the market (we must differentiate our product from their low cost offerings)

Anonymous

It is my first impression that some areas of the business have done a much better job of succession planning and managing the introduction of new talent into the organization. I feel we need to stress this more in the future, particularly in my area. I have gone to all of my peers and asked them their opinions of the marketing and sales finance area. The response was less than acceptable and that needs to be addressed. We also need to prepare on how to report the major product shifts we are going to have in 2010.

Anonymous

Replacing loss of experience and building a solid infrastructure for future capacity and capability to provide business leadership. Expand lead finance roles beyond reporting and analysis responsibilities (controllership) to include business leadership partnership (to be an integrated part of the decision making process by each business leader).

Anonymous

Managing productivity projects and achieving respective goals Mitigating the effect of commodity increases

Anonymous

1.Succession planning -while one of our strengths is experience, we have several key associates who could all possibly retire around the same time. We also have some associates who are very comfortable in their positions, don't want to move into others (out of fear or comfort in current role), so we aren't getting a lot of cross fertilization in the groups.

2. In 2010, we are in a major transition year and I'm concerned that we may have overlooked some things in our 2011 plan and reconciling our performance with our plan could be a major issue in 2010.

Anonymous

Succession planning not just for finance but in the operations group who we depend on for accurate data and process knowledge. Support and knowledge of the existing systems and their impact. Example the BOM issues for Toledo)

Anonymous

We have had many individuals transition to different assignments and have lost a great deal of knowledge about many aspects of the business. I believe we will have a lengthy learning curve to overcome this transition period.

Anonymous

SEER 13 introduction. The 2011 Plan is an aggressive plan. Investment and expense related capital still prove to be a huge challenge for the CCOE. We will be taking over the CCOE activities currently performed by Joy Watson, Houston Plant Accounting, in 1Q06 without adding any additional headcount. Due to the difficulty of current systems and lack of systems that talk to each other, the tracking of our capital spend is a nightmare. One which we have been handling with spreadsheets manually.

Who are the key customers of this organization and what are their demands?

Anonymous

Sales and Marketing and Manufacturing are the key customer internally. The external customer base is highly differentiated. In both cases, the customer has a "gimme what i need" button. Our job is to anticipate the need or at the least respond quickly. We could be serving our internal customers with more tailored analytical information.

Anonymous

IWD's & and higher-cost home builders -demand quality, reliability, timeliness of deliveries, and multiple configurations

Anonymous

While we must satisfy the needs of the corporation by preparing the highest quality work and reporting, I feel the most value is obtained in giving the sales and marketing management teams the highest quality of support possible. They are looking for better information of the industry and competitors. They want better access to expense information. They want more sharing of financial information of all types that help them do their jobs. They want more support in the development and measurement of business cases.

Anonymous

Corporate reporting and analysis. Demands are sometimes poorly scheduled or adhoc in nature and almost never fit the current alignment of reporting and analysis being performed for CS internal use. External Customers -our business partners (AMS Dealers and IWD distributors). We currently fall short of being the best in the eyes of our customers because our business reporting and customer service systems are not enterprise wide in nature but rather are aligned with our own internal reporting and business unit organizations (examples would be Residential, Commercial, Extended Warranty, Finance and Parts -no one stop customer service communication vehicle.

Anonymous

My customers are the site supply chain and finance leaders. They demand productivity numbers that are accurate and goals that are attainable. More importantly, they require updated communication regarding suppliers' prices, forecasts, demand shifts, etc. They demand perfection 110% of the time and I'm only at 105% :)

Anonymous

Our key customers are CS Business Leaders and Corporate Controllers. Business Leaders -we should be transitioning from scorekeepers to strategists, not just publishing results but providing analytics for future decisions, advice and counsel and to some extent, demand accountability. Corporate Controllers -besides standard

reporting requirements, we have an obligation to inform
them of any significant risks/ opportunities as we are aware of them.

Anonymous

Plant operations -timely data -SOX leadership -quality analysis. CS
HQ -quality of forecasts, analysis, support of SOX initiatives

Anonymous

The Business Leaders are the key customers. Their demands are
that we provide the service that they request -when they request it.
At times, they do not take into consideration the normal Finance
closing, forecast, or other required time constraints.

How well does the organization meet customer expectations?

Anonymous

I think we meet requirements, but I don't think we have impressed
the Leadership Team. We need to do more to provide them with new
products and improved products. We need to anticipate more and
have the answer before they ask.

Anonymous

I think our satisfaction rating is approx 85%

Anonymous

The marketing and sales organization is aware that we have five
open positions and that half of the remaining people are on the job
less than a year. There is a level of impatience that some critical
items are not available. We are working with HR to address these
items.

Anonymous

Organization has long history of meeting or exceeding expectations
through dedication and extra effort on the part of team members.

Anonymous

I think finance as an organization does a great job at
handling expectations. Often this takes a lot of extra hours,

though. In the end, if the numbers look good, finance will look good.

Anonymous

Business leaders -we do a very good job of publishing timely and accurate results. We need to improve and standardize our processes to give greater visibility to data and trends. We also need to improve our forward looking analysis. Corporate Controllers -I think we meet expectations in this area.

Anonymous

I give us a C. with the trend improving in the latter part of 2011. More communications and understanding developed between finance and operations on how we will operate and forecast our costs. However data is often too old. Problems with original 2011 budget preparation though identified was always a thorn as we had to explain ourselves repeatedly and finally dismissed a problem individual who was simply not responding.

Anonymous

Very well when it does not conflict with other Finance "Priorities" -closing, etc.

At what does this organization excel?

Anonymous

As I mentioned elsewhere, CS Finance is highly efficient, has strong controls, and provides timely information. I think CS Finance is the best organization of its kind in AMS.

Anonymous

Very good at producing a quality product that lasts for years, knowing the market (e.g. heavily into replacement and anticipating where it is going (e.g., complete home environment) -I am proud to work here because it was a world-class organization when I arrived and continues to be so (regardless of what some might say); historically we have treated our people in a way that other companies could only envy; our ethics in business; our creative solutions

Anonymous

My first impression is that they are extremely dedicated and will do whatever is required to meet objectives. They work very hard to pick up the slack for open positions. I am proud to be a member of a management team that is knowledgeable and respectful. I look forward to a very rewarding relationship with the team.

Anonymous

Producing a large volume of accurate analytical reporting to a broad and large audience in a compressed time frame.

Anonymous

We're good at listening to each other. I think we all feel like we're on the same team and we all are here for the same reason -which doesn't mean we can't challenge each other sometimes to be better.

Anonymous

Finance associates take a great deal of pride and responsibility in their work. However, I think we tend to take on more and more responsibilities without asking for additional resources (we're frugal by nature) and our work (or work/life balance) tends to suffer as a result. At the end of the Night, we do whatever it takes to meet deadlines.

Anonymous

Overall a leadership organization with a high level of ownership and accountability, that has started to turn a corner in the latter part of 2011. A plant that produces quality products that you can feel good about associating your name with.

Anonymous

We make our deadlines and due dates. We can absorb work -Sarbanes -Oxley requirements, and still survive -although we are probably stretching that envelop.

Anonymous

The CCOE (and CS) is good at execution. We continually meet CS (and AMS) expectations. I am proud to work for AMS because I think we are making a difference in the community in many ways but the most important in Safety. It is nice to work for a company that has integrity. CS Leadership has integrity and is perceived to have integrity. We set realistic goals and adhere to our AOP

How does this organization measure its performance?

Anonymous

The scorecard published by *Jan Brown* monthly is the only measurement of which I'm aware. However, since the scorecard has no effect on our compensation, it's largely ignored. I think you could influence our relevant VPs to incorporate some performance measurements but we would need to be able to affect the outcome.

Anonymous

Many different ways -too numerous to mention here

Anonymous

My first impression is that the PMP process is it. I want to expand on this in the future and provide meaningful metrics that are within people's control.

Anonymous

Monthly financial score card of reporting deadlines / accuracy of forecasting.

Anonymous

This is something we just started with a finance scorecard. We measure if our material is onetime and accurate vs. previous forecasts. I'm not sure if there are other intentions.

Anonymous

The finance scorecard was created to measure the "big two" areas that every finance person strives for -timeliness and accuracy. However, we need to measure the more intangible goal of becoming more CFO-like.

Anonymous

Are people progressing on their individual goals and our team goals, have we improved from the last quarter. What are our prime customer complaints and what are we doing about them.

Anonymous

Not sure.

Anonymous

We can get better. While we measure financial performance very well, I think there are productivity measurements that can be standardized. While I agree we should have a scorecard, I do not think it is a perfect metric for performance.

If you were in my position, what would you do first?

Anonymous

Get to know your customers and get to know your people so you can serve your customers better with the right people.

Anonymous

Slit my throat (just kidding!!) -Get to know your direct reports; give credence to what they say; support their needs; and watch them support your (and the organization's) needs, goals, and aspirations (we'll help you look great if you will give us a chance) -Balance the workload (some locations are overstaffed -others are understaffed)

Anonymous

I would do the same thing you are doing, getting to know the people and the business. I would stress getting the best possible people for open positions and measure managers and HR on getting those openings filled.

Anonymous

Understand how the existing financial organization is functioning -who does what and why. Shore up holes (backfills/training) and transitional transfer of process/procedural knowledge issues ASAP.

Anonymous

I think I would do pretty much what you've done so far -reiterate the fact that the organization has performed very well, you aren't out to make any radical changes (At least until you are more familiar with us), and continue to stay positive in general.

Anonymous

Let finance know that you care about them as people, not as the hired help. Listen to them and be seen as someone who actually understands what they do, the effort it takes to do it, and support them in their requests.

Anonymous

Communicate your expectations (hot buttons), vision for the organization. Roles and responsibilities between Jan and Tim, where do the site finance people fit.

Anonymous

Try to get an understanding of the overall business and how all the pieces fit together.

Anonymous

Focus on Materials productivity and replace ProTrak. Organization Vision: Direct Reports

Do you understand the vision driving the organization?

Anonymous

NO -I don't believe Finance has a vision that is different from the short term business goal of max income and cash generation. Not even sure what we would do with a vision statement.

Anonymous

I believe the letter that Dave sent out for the 2011 plan articulated what the primary drivers for 2011 are.
• Achieve premier customer service.
• Drive operational excellence.
• Deliver business plan results.
• Invest in our people – people make it happen.

Anonymous

Yes. In simple terms -drive the top line, drive the bottom line, and the market will reward you

Anonymous
> Clearly understand vision driving; not the structure and mechanisms to envisioned to achieve vision.

Anonymous
> I'm not sure if there's a secondary vision besides ensuring that our numbers are accurate, on time, and in compliance with SarBox.

Anonymous
> I knew what John Smith's vision was for Finance. I would like to know if Smith shares the same vision or what his vision will be.

Anonymous
> We develop our site and department goals to tie into the strategic goals for CS. We tailor specific strategies for Toledo to be competitive with our sister plants and external competition. We feel we have a road to climb being in the North East and what we fell are perceptions people may have with manufacturing here. Finance has to help reduce and control our costs not be a passive reporter.

Anonymous
> I believe I have a good understanding of the vision of CS in total. Not sure I understand the Finance Vision.

Anonymous
> Yes. Be the best in the eyes our cusomers, employees and shareowners.

Do you think others understand the vision driving the organization?

Anonymous
> No idea but probably not.

Anonymous
> The goal setting process we will be going through over the next few weeks should clarify any issues that people have about our objectives.

Anonymous

Many do

Anonymous

Yes

Anonymous

If the vision is above then yes. If there's additional visions, I'm not too sure.

Anonymous

They know to the extent the vision aligns with CS total vision. Allen was not as open with all of finance as to his vision except that he wanted everyone to become more CFO like and less scorekeepers.

Anonymous

The Leadership commmunicates with staff on the vision and seeks inputs. I think people know and understand the vision for the plant and the department. They have seen a lot of change this past year. Responses in any facility and group will be mixed, from those who are looking to retire to those looking for advancement.

Anonymous

I believe individuals understand the CS vision -not sure people understand the Finance Vision.

Anonymous

I think we understand the vision but do question how we are doing it. One example I have heard recently refers to "We recognize the importance of our people". If we recognize their importance, then why are so many being hired from the outside? Why are we so quick to hire from the outside rather than develop the talent we have?

What changes do we need to make in order to achieve our future?

Anonymous

I don't know what our future is. Nevertheless, I believe in the next ten years, this business will need to evolve to meet serious challenges pertaining to the effects and sources of global warming, cost of power, pollution and shifts in global power. This will mean we will need to evolve our financial capabilities to accomodate broader, more differentiated products, more product integration, different distribution and sourcing methods and an international product scope. Our financial systems will have to change and we need to get smart on how to do that. We will need to be more flexible, quicker and more efficient. We will need to move the application of our human resource away from data processing to analysis and advice.

Anonymous

Stay on the cutting edge of technology whether it is product, systems, or human resources

Anonymous

I think I am too new to recommend changes. I do believe that we have to focus on our people and make sure they have the guidance and the tools to do their job.

Anonymous

Need to carry organizational vision down to aligned communication at operational level to make certain that vision of how to operationalize into actionable, measurable goals for individuals as well as developmental plans. Need more than a 1 to 2% incremental economic incentive to individuals to contribute above and beyond the call of duty to make things happen. Our current organization and compensation structures tend to promote team work and group think rather than giving specific and timely recognition and reward for individual's contributions, resulting in people sitting in a position that they are "good at" for LONG times. Need additional focus and challenge to develop internal bench strength of existing finance personnel through continued education / developmental plans that encourage growth. Change finance to a place in the organization that people want to work.

Anonymous

We need to continue the team work, be able to openly challenge each other, and most importantly, we willing to change when change is necessary.

Anonymous

I believe investments in information technology (modifying existing systems or developing new systems) will be the key change needed to achieve my goals for finance.

Anonymous

Get the basics right and the data accurate, standardize on metrics. We can not talk about six sigma when the base data is flawed and there are too many sources or interpritations of the data.

Anonymous

Not sure.

Anonymous

We need to share best practices in order to consistenly provide only the necessary data for metric reporting. We need to invest in continuing training for our Finance folks which should provide immediate productivity improvements. We need to use Six Sigma for process improvements.

Are we staffed and resourced appropriately to accomplish the organization's mission?

Anonymous

Over the next few years, continuing a trend already in progress, some highly experienced people will retire and, before that happens, finance needs to bring in and train the replacements by developing entry level jobs that are attractive and career paths that entice people to remain with us and grow. Hiring "experienced" professionals doesn't get us the same mindset and doesn't assure the present dedication to controls, systems and analysis.

Anonymous

Not yet. I have 4 open positions at this time and one position where I have issues due to illness. I may also have one individual who may need some additional coaching that will need to be addressed. This is my largest challenge going into next year.

Anonymous

In most cases, yes. We have done an excellent job at the top (especially in CS). I'd like to see it become less difficult at my level to make the needed changes (especially if they involve adding human resources).

Anonymous

Yes and No. Yes; Generally people doing their jobs are adequate at what they are doing and have been in their positions a long time [Associates tend to know what they know and don't have interest or time to go beyond that]. No; There has recently been and continues to be an infusion of new personnel without adequate transitional planning and training by out going personnel. Little or no cross training or sharing of process/procedural expertise has occurred. Due to losses of capacity as well as capability, we are currently struggling with learning curves in order to accomplish the everyNight processing and analysis that our customers have come to expect as well as the recently added auditing/documentation compliance with Sox, leaving little or no ability to provide for real gain in productivity or process improvement (Deployment of Six Sigma tools; Development of new metrics and additional analytics). [No resource to direct and groom the forest for putting out all the fires on the individual trees] No; Lack of visibility and awareness to the processes of CS finance fit together and how what associates do effects the financial organization. There is no well defined and widely communicated career path in CS finance. [Don't realize that they don't know what they don't know].

Anonymous

I think for the most part we do (although this role is the first time I've really been involved in finance!)

Anonymous

Not in all cases. We have upgraded talent in many key areas but we have C player in some roles. However, these are long term, hard working, very dedicated employees. It's difficult to phase them out of a role.

Anonymous

Not 100% but we are getting there with our new hires and pulling in tasks from other groups to have the entire picture in our view.

Anonymous

In Finance -I believe we do not have experienced individuals in many of the key positions in the Finance group. I'm sure they will mature with time, but we could be without important information or understanding for a while.

Anonymous

For the most part, yes. I think over the last year, we have invested in financial expertise but we are still faced with the learning curve of understanding our business. I do think there are some key individuals that carry some of our processes and we need to capture their knowledge before some of them retire or leave the company. In the CCOE, we have hired two new team member in Dallas and we moved one of our finance team members from Dallas to Superior temporarily to facilitate the financial transition of moving scrolls which is giving her international experience. I also have a Houston analyst who is currently working on her accounting degree and three Dallas employees who are taking English classes.

Chapter Five: Managing Leadership Transitions To Build A Learning Culture

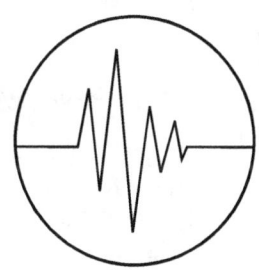

Executive Summary For Chapter Five

Leadership transitions within organizations present a significant opportunity to promote real learning. The primary message of this chapter is that for e-Learning to realize its promise it is necessary to address the current organizational culture and its view of the learner. The technologies available to support e-Learning are merely tools with which to address the deeper cultural issues that inhibit learning in most corporate settings.

The chapter offers a critique of the banking approach to learning and development in which content is deposited into the learner who is seen as an empty pot. In its place a constructivist view of learning is presented which supports the type of learning that takes place in today's emerging communities of practice. E-learning technologies can be an effective means of promoting the emergence of communities of practice

Leadership transitions within organizations present a significant opportunity to promote real learning as.well as communities of practice. Transitions also lend themselves to the use of intelligently designed e-learning tools. A properly designed leadership transition program is a practical way to implement an effective approach to learning, thereby initiating a change in organizational culture. The chapter suggests that this change concentrate on current management behaviors in the context of a systemic approach to leadership transition and management changes in general. It also describes a specific Leadership Transition System (LTS) that is consistent with effective approaches to learning and the learner. This System is available with all of its components from *Leadership Transition Solutions*.

Introduction

A senior executive of a major pharmaceutical company, responsible for leading the organization's effort to define its e-Learning strategy, recently made this observation: "The good news is that senior management has discovered e-Learning. And the bad news is that senior management has discovered e-Learning." Explaining his observation, he indicated that the expectations held by senior management for the ability of technology to both reduce the cost of training and raise its quality were seriously unrealistic. By being overly enamored of technology, leadership was ignoring the more important obstacles to learning. These include an inappropriate view of the learner and the learning process, cultures built on command and control orientations to the employee that inhibit development, and training models based on an overemphasis on content as an end in itself.

Technology has become the tail wagging the dog in the e-Learning marketplace. The real issues are not related to technology; the real issues have to do with corporate cultures that have been subjected to forces that severely limit the ability of individuals to learn and develop on the job. If e-Learning is to take us to organizational cultures in which real human development occurs daily at the workbench, then action must be taken to develop these cultures. In the interest of a campaign to realize this new land, we can begin by saying simply: "It's the culture, stupid!"

This is not to say that technology has no place in corporate learning. In fact, the Internet and the technology of the Web and Web-based applications are directly supportive of a learning culture. The World Wide Web has emerged as the basis for learning and knowledge generation, as well as a source of transformational change for traditional learning institutions and mechanisms. The training and development function in corporate organizations is being deeply challenged by the reality of the Web and its technologies. But the value of these technologies will only be realized when corporate cultures become learning cultures.

A major premise of this chapter is that current corporate cultures treat the learner as an empty pot to be filled, an outdated and rejected view of how adults learn. Adults know and learn in the exercise of reflection and action on the world. They practice this reflection and action on a daily basis in clearly defined communities within corporate organizations. These communities of practice are just beginning to be appreciated in relation to their central role in the organization and its ongoing learning.

However, the prevailing view of the learner as an empty pot continues to be expressed in most of the formal structures of learning and their continuing emphasis on the transferring of content (filling the pot.) This chapter will provide a review of the literature on adult learning theory and identify those theories that have value for corporate efforts to develop cultures that support adult development. The work of Paulo Freire and others will be cited for its importance in providing a more accurate view of the adult learner and the process of human development.

In the final section we will suggest a method of cultural action that supports learning and knowledge generation within specific communities of practice. This method seeks to change corporate cultures in the interest of real human development and adult education by way of an integrated approach to leadership transitions and management changes in general. The method includes a Web-based leadership transition system, which is an e-Learning tool that helps to transform management behavior. Rather than being seen as an end in itself, the tool needs to be positioned as a means for changing an organization's culture in the interest of learning. When this is understood, the overall process for the design, development, installation and implementation of the technology can then be used as a major opportunity for organizational development and culture change.

Web-based Technologies and Learning

E-mail, social networking sites, blogs, Web sites, corporate portals and all the other Internet technologies that have emerged in the last five years have changed the nature of communication and the manner in which knowledge is generated and exchanged. We are all connected now to numerous networks or webs in which we communicate and have access to information and knowledge. Many of these webs continue to be invisible within  the formal corporate organization in spite of the crucial role that they play in knowledge generation and exchange. For example, a group of employees decide to meet weekly over lunch to discuss their growing collaboration in serving the needs of a major customer. They come from many different departments and functions, but their collaboration is not recognized in any organization chart. However, their contribution to customer service is substantial.

The primary challenge to corporate organizations is learning to take advantage of the activities of these webs without trying to control them. Efforts to control often lead to the disappearance of the web and its activities. To use the example of the group meeting weekly for lunch, a management intervention could well lead to a dampening of the creativity of the group and a suppression of the natural leadership that was being expressed within the group.

Positive work is emerging in relation to the type of web being called a community of practice. Communities of practice are groups of people informally bound together by shared expertise and passion for a joint enterprise – engineers engaged in the development of complex networks, sales professionals who specialize in strategic sales. The following chart (Wenger and Snyder, 2000, p.7) compares the community of practice with other types of work groups in corporate organizations.

Type of Group	Purpose	Who belongs	What holds it together?	How long does it last?
Community of Practice	To Develop members capabilities, to build and exchange knowledge	Individuals who select themselves	Passion, commitment and identification with group's expertise	As long as there is interest in maintaining the group
Formal Work Group	To deliver a product or service	Everyone who reports to the group's manager	Job requirements and goals	Until the next organization
Project Team	To accomplish a specific task	Employees assigned by management	The project milestones and goals	Until the project has been completed
Informal Network	To Collect and pass on information	Friends and business acquaintances	Mutual needs	As long as people have a reason to connect

Wenger and Snyder (Ibid., p.17-20) articulate the following ways in which communities of practice add value to organizations:

- They transfer best practices.

- They help drive strategy.

- They develop professional skills.

- They start new lines of business.

- They help companies recruit and retain

- They solve problems quickly.

Clearly, the promotion of communities of practice constitutes an effective way to develop both the organization and its talent. An effective method for such promotion is to design and develop Web-based applications that extend and enhance the ability of communities of practice to exchange knowledge.

Learning to Enhance Job Performance

One of the salient features of these communities is the manner in which they support learning. In the context of these communities, the individual is actively seeking out the knowledge, skills and abilities that are required to enhance and improve the practices of the community as well as personal performance. Learning occurs in conversations, e-mail exchanges, daily efforts at continuous improvement and focus on customers. Most significantly, learning is integrated with the daily effort to improve one's performance on the job.

If the technologies associated with e-Learning can be applied to support the individual in the daily effort to improve personal performance, the potential for e-Learning will be realized.

If we examine the research available on the nature of adult learning, we can identify further clues for the effective application of e-Learning technologies. The following section of this chapter provides a review of the literature on adult learning.

Adult Learning Theory

Traditional corporate adult education has borrowed concepts from pedagogical theory, modeling educational experiences on traditional classrooms and ignoring the different emotional, psychological and contextual concerns of the adult learner. A pragmatic attitude has prevailed as schools and industries have required increasingly more complex and specialized knowledge. Our schools must not only create skilled workers, they must also influence those workers' attitudes in a way that supports the "technological superstructure within which adult labor is organized" (Heaney, 1995).

This view of education was most eloquently challenged in the early 1970's with the publication of Paulo Freire's <u>Pedagogy of the Oppressed</u>, which argues that education as we know it inhibits creativity and the expansion of consciousness, thereby limiting the possibility of action for social change (Ibid).

Paulo Freire's emphasis on dialogue as the basis of informal education has significantly influenced thinking about progressive educational practices, especially as they relate to adult learners. Freire emphasized that education should not be about one person (the teacher, trainer or manager) acting upon another (the student or employee), but rather a process of people working with each other. He challenged the idea that learners are empty pots to be filled, calling that view of education a "banking" system in which educators (managers) made "deposits" into educatees (employees). Furthermore, Freire believed that education wasn't simply about deepening understanding; rather it should be about making a difference in the world through informed action--praxis --action built on values (Smith, 2001).

While Freire focused a great deal of attention on oppressed people, on the poor and under-educated, the implication of Freire's work for corporate educational systems and the culture that supports them is immense.

If corporations would stop trying to fill their employees with information as if they were empty pots and instead began to help employees liberate their creativity, enhance their problem-solving skills and empower them to act on their knowledge, we would have a corporate educational system and culture that would be consistent with the needs of communities of practice.

The behavior of individuals within specific communities of practice is consistent with the view of the learner that is inherent in the work of Friere and other experts on the adult learner. We will look at some of the themes that make up the bulk of adult educational theory and how they relate to the task of employee education within the corporate world.

Adult education literature generally supports the idea that adult learners need to be in learner-centered situations, setting their own goals and organizing their study around their current life needs (Imel, 1995). How one creates educational models around these needs is of course the question.

Classroom activities, as most of us have experienced for ourselves, are usually individually performed. Even when students do engage in small group work, their performance is individually judged. The lessons are generally detached from the learners' real-life situations and communities. This differs significantly from the modern world of work, where businesses have become performance driven and where much emphasis is put on collaboration, teamwork, and interpersonal communication skills.

Work in the corporate world is not only a shared activity, it is performed in a social setting in which what one can accomplish is based on what others are achieving (Brown, 1998, p.8). As such, most adult learning is experiential --it occurs within a real-life setting where the content of what needs to be learned is applicable in the environment in which it is learned. What is the role of the educator in such a system? How does this role differ from the traditional "banking" system that Freire critiqued? And what should this tell us about learning in a corporate setting? An exploration of constructivism, a major experiential learning theory, will help us find the answers to these questions.

Constructivism

Constructivism specifies that learning is best accomplished through interactions and experiences in one's environment (Brown, 1998, p.9). Based on understandings from developmental psychology, constructivism argues that people make meaning through personal interpretations of their interactions in the social environment. Prior experience and knowledge are important factors in the learning process and form the basis of future actions (Ibid., p 6). Constructivism "focuses the learner's attention on the 'why' of learning" and fosters critical thinking and intellectual development (Ibid., p7).

Constructivism has gained support based on current research in teaching and learning. The theory furthers the work of Piaget and Vygotsky, both psychologists who demonstrated that learners use different styles and methods to construct understandings. Vygotsky's work stresses the importance of learning in context. Constructivism represents a significant paradigm shift from the top-down, banking model of education that Freire argued against to a learner-centered approach to education (Ibid., p7). In constructivism the main goal of teaching is the empowerment of the learner. Teachers provide students with opportunities to reflect upon and test new theories in real experiences (Ibid., p8). Constructivism "promotes an 'examined life' and encourages the critical reflection of values, beliefs, and assumptions (Ibid.)."

Three key characteristics of constructivism are:

1. Cognition occurs as people share their understandings with each other and test the degree to which they are compatible.

2. The goal or purpose of investigation influences what is learned and what experiences the learner draws upon to construct new understandings.

3. Knowledge evolves through social negotiation, either independently or in collaborative groups. Alternative views and additional information enable learners to test the viability of understandings and to build new propositions that are compatible with those understandings (Ibid., p7).

Constructivism is a particularly well-suited theory for creating workplace educational models and it is directly supportive of learning within communities of practice. New theories, of course, imply new practices. A constructivist approach implies changes in instruction, curriculum and assessment. We will briefly outline these practical considerations.

Instruction

Instruction in a constructionist model requires new ways of using time, which in the old model is dictated by teachers, administrators, and in the workplace, by managers. The new paradigm calls for time for learners to work together to do some in-depth investigations of issues; they need to be able to spend time problem-solving and testing out  their newfound knowledge in the context of their lives (in our case, in the context of their community of practice). Instructors also need some time with individuals (Ibid., p18).

As learners create their own knowledge, the constructivist educator is more a mentor, coach and guide than a teacher. The constructivist educator learns along with the student. As co-learners they determine together the course of instruction, the goals and objectives of their time together. The use of experts to coach learners is a key strategy, and coaching is gradually removed as the learner gains in experience and expertise. Vygotsky calls this process scaffolding which supports the learner as he moves to the edge of his ability, and like scaffolding on a skyscraper, slowly allows the learner to go beyond his former limitations (Ibid., p18-19).

If managers can be influenced to see themselves as constructivist educators or coaches, especially in the context of their management of individual performance, an organization can begin to develop a real learning culture.

Another instructional element is the need to engage the learner in "reflective thought and action" (Ibid.). The learner must be asked, and be asking herself, what has meaning for her. She must have the chance (the time) to reflect on what she has been doing and what she is learning. Feedback from others is a central part of this self-reflective process (Ibid.). In this context, the use of structured feedback can take on new meaning and effectiveness in the overall development of the individual. Feedback during the transition process into a new set of responsibilities can be especially productive of deep personal learning.

Curriculum

A constructivist curriculum is contextual; learning must be linked with real life (real work) experience and new knowledge must be tested out in workplace applications. Curriculum must provide multiple perspectives and reflect the complexities of the workplace environment, emphasizing interdisciplinary learning and the interrelatedness of seemingly different concepts. The focus must be on the construction of knowledge, not the reproduction of it (Ibid., pp. 19-20).

Of central importance, the curriculum must include perceptual, cognitive, and affective dimensions. Learners' diverse backgrounds and experiences, beliefs and attitudes, will lead them to seek knowledge in different ways. Learning styles are different, although most involve some aspect of the perceptual --learning through the senses, through experiencing, doing and being involved. People process information differently and the curriculum needs to allow for the cognitive cycle.

In this cycle the learner moves from concrete experience to reflection and observation, to abstract conceptualization and lastly to active experimentation.

The Cognitive Cycle of Learning

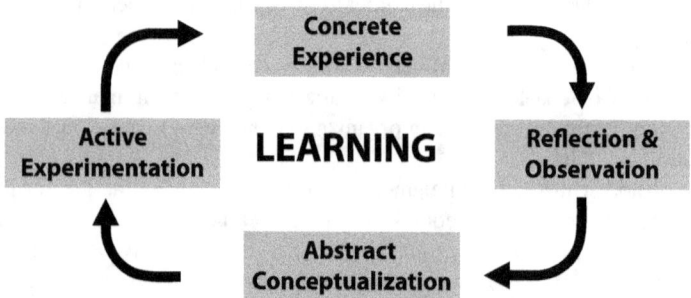

The affective dimension demands that people have a place to express their feelings and their values, and allows for different modes of behavior. Collaborative efforts give learners a chance to hear from each other and come to appreciate different viewpoints (Ibid., pp. 20-21). In this context, the learner creates his own curriculum by reaching for resources needed on a daily basis to carry out the work at hand and improve one's performance in doing so.

Assessment

Assessment in a constructivist model must take into account what the learner himself feels he has accomplished. Testing and evaluations give way to self-monitoring, reflection, peer-review and feedback. Portfolios and journals may be used to demonstrate the ground the student has covered. Developing standards and measurement criteria is an important challenge for the constructivist educator, and assessments must offer opportunities for additional learning.

The focus of assessment is not a question of comparison to others, but rather a reflection on what is learning, how it is done, and how it can be improved (Ibid. pp. 22-23).

Constructivist Learning in the Workplace

Workplace learning is highly suited to a constructivist approach. Informal, incidental learning takes place in all work environments; it is how people 'learn the ropes'. When starting a new job, most people learn the job as they do it, while reflecting on what they accomplish, what they need to do better, and what they think they need to know. Being guided by experts and interacting with other workers plays a key role in the acquiring of knowledge. Repeated opportunities for problem-solving reinforces what is learned as workers gain experience and confidence (Kerka, 1997, p.2).

Natural elements of the workplace make it an excellent environment for fostering a constructivist approach to learning. These include real, goal-directed activities; access to guidance from peers, experts, and incidental cues from the environment; every-day problem-solving; and reinforcement that comes about from the process (Ibid.).

Making the Most of Leadership Transitions Using E-Learning

The corporate practices related to leadership transition have been in place for a good ten years. The process is often referred to as executive assimilation and General Electric is well-known as having perfected the process and made it a systematic element of their management transitions. The process involves interviewing key individuals related to the new manager and assembling his/her team in a meeting designed to introduce people to each other and begin to identify the key issues facing the new manager. For the most part, these activities tend to be informal and sometimes they are effective and sometimes they are superficial. Because of the hit and miss nature of how programs are carried out, the opportunity for learning in the transition seldom reaches its potential.

An effective leadership transition process requires a few essential elements. The requirements of an effective process are presented in the following graphic:

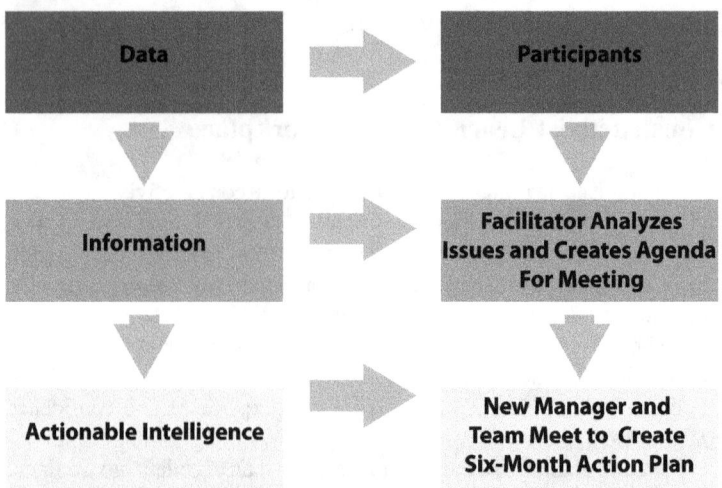

An Ideal Setting for the Application of e-Learning

The data gathering and generation of information that are essential elements in the leadership transition process lend themselves to the use of an interactive, web-based application. Instead of having to rely on informal interviews that are time-consuming and inefficient, it is possible to construct highly refined interview schedules that are easily accessible via the Internet. These interviews can take the form of Worksheets that are designed for each category of participant. The data that they produce then provides a substantial source of comprehensive information about the organization in which the new manager is taking on a new role. The

150

result is a 360 degree view of the organization that is produced quickly and efficiently. The Worksheets can be assigned to participants in all of the key roles surrounding a new manager. The graphic below illustrates the key roles surrounding a new manager identified as John Adams.

Organization Chart for John Adams

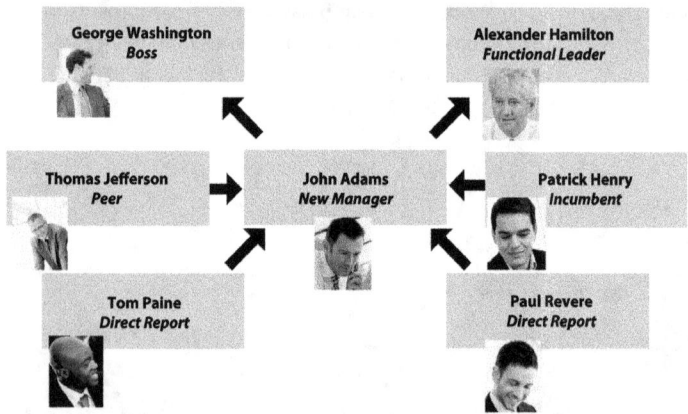

Once the Worksheets are completed there can be selective interviewing of participants to probe and expand on the key issues that emerge in the Worksheets. Worksheets can be customized and allow for confidential responses.

The interaction with Worksheets on the part of all of the key participants in a leadership transition process supports learning that honors the three characteristics of constructivism mentioned earlier:

- Cognition occurs as people share their understandings with each other and test the degree to which they are compatible.

- The goal or purpose of investigation influences what is learned and what experiences the learner draws upon to construct new understandings.

- Knowledge evolves through social negotiation, either independently or in collaborative groups. Alternative views and additional information enable learners to test the viability of understandings and to build new propositions that are compatible with those understandings.

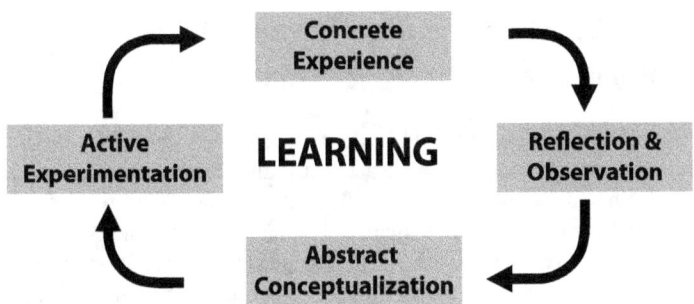

The leadership transition process also provides an ideal setting for the cognitive cycle of learning to take place as the graphic below illustrates.

The concrete experience is the transition itself, the Worksheets and the team meeting support refined reflection and observation, the six-month action plan is the resulting abstract conceptualization and its implementation is the active experimentation. Given this exceptional potential for learning on the part of both the new manager and the organization, the leadership transition event should become a systemic element of an overall leadership development strategy. The use of a web-based technology platform applied consistently to management transitions is a powerful means of ensuring both learning and consistently successful startups for new managers.

Creative Customization of Worksheets and Data-mining Potential

The web-based Worksheets that are the core of the e-Learning application being described here can be customized for unique situations. They can also be analyzed over time to identify key trends and issues that are occurring across the organization. Organization development issues can be effectively identified as multiple management changes provide the opportunity for hundreds of individuals to be interviewed using the Worksheets.

Appendix A is a report that resulted from the use of a customized Worksheet. It shows the potential for stimulating communities of practice as a result of the learning that can take place during a leadership transition. The report is the result of a thoughtful District Manager for a major manufacturing company asking four of his peers some key questions about their own startup experience. A single Worksheet was sent to these four individuals and the report presents their responses.

153

Facilitation of the Transition Meeting and the Transition Coach

The web-based, e-Learning application that supports the data gathering and information generation aspects of the transition process is complemented by the work of the Transition Coach. The role of this individual is to assist the new manager in the analysis of the Worksheet results to identify key issues, create the Agenda for the Transition Meeting with the team and to facilitate this meeting. The primary objectives of the meeting are to bring the new manager and the team together and to create a six-month action plan that is owned by both the new manager and the team. When the facilitation work is done skillfully, the manager has the support of a strong mentor or coach to whom he can turn for support during his/her first months on the job. Clearly, the role of the Transition Coach is as important as the role of the e-Learning application. Together they provide an effective high-tech and high-touch combination in support of real learning.

Summary and Conclusions

There is enormous potential for learning in the leadership transition moment. The importance of transitions has been effectively articulated by the work of Michael Watkins. His five propositions about transition effectively state this importance.

Five Propositions About Leadership Transitions

- The root causes of transition failure always lie in a pernicious interaction between the situation, with its opportunities and pitfalls, and the individual, with his or her strengths and vulnerabilities.

- There are systematic methods that leaders can employ to both lessen the likelihood of failure and reach the break even point faster.

- The overriding goal in a transition is to build momentum by creating virtuous cycles that built creditability and by avoiding getting caught in vicious cycles that damage credibility.

- Transitions are a crucible for leadership development and should be managed accordingly.

- Adoption of a standard framework for accelerating transitions can yield big returns for organizations.

The adoption of a standard framework for accelerating transitions is essentially what this chapter has been describing in recommending the use of a web-based e-Learning application. Such an application provides the foundation for a systematic approach to transition and makes sure its potential for learning is fully realized. The transition process is too important to be left to informal and hit and miss methods. With the intelligent combination of technology and skillful coaching, an organization can begin to create a real learning culture through its approach to leadership transitions.

Appendix A

Learning from the Leadership Transition Challenges Facing New District Managers in the Ajax Commercial Systems (ACS) Organization

This report was developed using the Leadership Transition Program Website located at www.leadershiptransitions.net. A customized Worksheet was created to support a new District Manager who will be assuming responsibilities in January, 2011. The Worksheet posed questions to four peers of this District Manager, who had assumed the same role within ACS during the past year. These four individuals completed the assigned Worksheet during the month of December.

The report that follows was generated by William F. Pilder, site administrator, using the Summary Reporting functionality that is available in *Dialogue™*. It contains a number of thoughtful ideas and suggestions that should be useful to any individual assuming the role of District Manager within ACS.

Responses to Startup Assessment Questions Posed to Four Peers of the Incoming District Manager

What are the most important understandings

developed from your first months on the job?

1. Peer One
Being "The Leader" is different than being a leader. You have been through this, so this should not be an issue in your particular district.

2. Peer Two
It is important to understand the current concerns and issues with all the associates. This can be done through a set of assimilation meetings. They provide insight into what is working and what is not. You will also learn who your natural leaders are. You also should do an assessment of your current Leadership Team. I would ask each of your Leadership Team members to put together their assessment of the business. This will provide insight into their ability to work as a team. I provide insight to your opportunities.

3. Peer Three
The book "The first 90 days " was key to my transition being successful. I spent the first 90 days executing the plans in the book . Some of the details were to perform "Skip-a-level" meetings with many of the associates. I also looked at each business within the business to determine if it is in a Start up, Turn Around, Realignment, or Sustain mode. I then gauged my degree of change management, collective decision making, and level of "loose-tight" control. As an example, I determined that the contracting organization was a turnaround candidate and moved quick, placed resources in a "command and control" manner, made most of the tough personnel calls myself, set quick short term expectations. As a contrast, the Service organization was determined to be a "re-alignment" while they all thought it was a "sustain". As a result, I had to use lots of "other Ajax office" info to set a case that we weren't as great as we thought we were. Now our goals are more stretch and reach than they were in the past.

4. Peer Four
People, culture and community

What were the most significant challenges in your first six months?

1. Peer One
Getting to know a new leadership team, assessing their Strengths and Weaknesses. Trying to understand the "History and Culture" of the organization. performing a solid assessment of where the office really was in terms of performance and capabilities. Then creating an agenda that can move the organization forward.

2. Peer Two
The most challenging issue I had was to build a strong Leadership team that could work together and carryout the vision of the organization. You will most likely find that you have several weak areas on your team that need addressing. The other challenge that I had was addressing improper accounting practices from the previous Controller. This put a lot of financial pressure on the office for the first six months. Another challenge that you will have is transitioning from the previous manager's style to yours, especially if there is a significant difference. There will be a lot of resistance from parts of the organization that was used to not having much engagement from the District Manager.

3. Peer Three
Biggest challenge was implementing change while the person I'm succeeding is still involved in the business. Many things to be changed were designed, implemented, and "owned" by the former leader. I have to move slower as a result to ensure harmony and non-mutinous behavior is demonstrated. I also had a manager who was very strong but left a wake when dealing with others. I've sent him to CCL and things are turning around. Also many were unsure of who I was and what I stand for. As a result, in addition to the skip-a-levels, I started circulating a weekly newsletter (My Perspective) which ensured that those who read it knew what I was thinking, what my top 5 priorities are, and how we are doing on achieving them. I am now on my 48th week of publishing this to the troops.

4. Peer Four
being accepted in a new culture and gaining respect and establishing credibility.

What would you do differently if you had the chance to start again?

1. Peer One
Perform structured interviews
with entire leadership team, one
on one. Perform one or two skip
level interviews. Meet with more
customers to determine their view
of the organization.

2. Peer Two
I would have spent more time with our customers and getting
feedback from them. I would do a better
job of communicating with our associates on a regular basis.

3. Peer Three
Not too much, other than having accepted a 3 year transition plan. 3
years is too long. Other than that,
perhaps I would have spent a little more time getting to know my
leadership team personally - family
dinners, team building, etc. Also, I missed the fact that there was a
lot of history and resultant agendas
among my team. They had preconceived ideas of who should/could/
would do what rather than look at
the process of business and determining the proper responsibilities.

4. Peer Four
Spent more time gaining trust

Are there any aspects of your job responsibilities that you would like to change?

1. Peer One
No

2. Peer Two

I believe that there are currently too many internal demands being put on the District Manager by
Corporate. It is diverting our attention from focusing on the customer and the overall business.

3. Peer Three

None, I like the General Management requirements of the job.

4. Peer Four

yes - too many direct reports, not enough time for personnel development

Do you think your job is properly structured within the overall ACS organization?

1. Peer One

Yes...we're still working through the territory support
structure. At times the chain of command can be
confusing to our associates.

2. Peer Two

Yes and No. I believe that we are expected to run our office from a business perspective and are being
held accountable for delivering results. But I also believe that there is too much micro managing going
on today in regards to making financial and HR decisions. This is impacting our ability to effectively
make decisions and be seen as the leader of our business. We should have more freedom to make
unilateral day to day decisions and be held accountable for our performance.

3. Peer Three

Yes, However, I am concerned about rumblings of continually chipping away at both the reduction of the responsibilities of a DM and the commensurate rewards. This is a true "Intrapreneur" position and should remain that way, so long as initiatives and goals from corporate are met.

4. Peer Four
yes

What specific advice can you give me to make my startup effective?

1. Peer One
See item 2.

2. Peer Two
Develop continuity with your Leadership team. This will be critical as you implement change in the organization. I would also recommend prioritizing the issues that need to be accomplished. Make sure to celebrate your victories. Also provide updates to all associates on how things are going. This will keep them in tune with your vision.

3. Peer Three
1. READ THE BOOK - The First 90 Days - Michael Watkins 2. Do what's in the Book 3. Do Skip a level meetings - make sure your management team knows the purpose and the unyielding need for you to do these. 4. Find a communication vehicle that is easy, short, frequent that makes you real.

4. Peer Four
Stick to the basics that were the foundation of your success in CT. Those people skills will be the reason for your continued success.

Are there any particular activities that I should do with my direct reports as I take over my new job?

1. Peer One
From reading the first 90 days, I wouldn't do a lot of team building exercises until I had my final team assembled. I made changes to my team, after going through OT teambuilding exercises. It made the time and money investment less rewarding than if we'd waited until I had my team assembled.

2. Peer Two
I would recommend a group assimilation meeting facilitated by someone else and then I would conduct one on one interviews with each of them to understand what each of them thinks is important fro you to address in the business. I would also establish a vision with them that they can deliver throughout the organization. I would also establish what your expectations of them are and how you are going to hold them accountable. This might be different from the last manager.

3. Peer Three
I strongly suggest a CCL team-building session, or refresher if they've been through it. You also may want to have each of them write a "mock" business plan for the entire business -it will flush their agendas. Finally, I would make sure that they are taking full advantage of the PDP/PMP process, not just sleep walking through it. It will greatly help you in getting to know them and in helping them meet your expectations.

4. Peer Four
Let them see that you are a real person. Invite them to your home and invite them into your life.

Recommended Practices for New District Managers in Their First 90 Days

The following recommendations are culled from the preceding material. They constitute a set of potentially valuable practices for District Managers in the ABC organization to use during the first months on the job. They also could be the start of creating an ongoing dialogue among District Managers within ABC about how to support each other as a community of practice. Finding concrete ways to support this ongoing dialogue will create a community of practice that will improve both personal and organizational performance.

- Conduct a thorough assessment of your leadership team by performing structured interviews with each member.

- Ask each member of your leadership team to put together an assessment of the business.

- Learn who your key customers are and try to visit them to introduce yourself.

- Read The First 90 Days by Michael Watkins and follow its recommendations closely, especially performing "skip-a-level" meetings and assessing each business within the business to determine if it is in a Start-up, Turn Around, Realignment or Sustain mode.

- Create a weekly newsletter which ensures that those who read it know what you are thinking, what your top five priorities are and how the organization is doing in terms of achieving them.

- Make sure to celebrate your victories.

- Conduct a group assimilation meeting facilitated by a third party.

- Conduct one-on-one interviews with direct reports, peers,

your boss and customers to determine what the key issues are facing the organization and prepare an agenda for the group assimilation meeting based on these interviews. The website tool: www.leadershiptransitions.net provides an efficient way to conduct these interviews using specially designed Worksheets that you can customize.

- Conduct a Center for Creative Leadership team-building session following the group assimilation meeting or as part of this meeting.

- Take full advantage of the PDP/PMP process as it will greatly help you in getting to know the individual members of your team.

- Find ways for your team to get to know you personally.

Bibliography

Ideas for Leaders

The Checklist Manifesto: How to Get Things Right, Atul Gawande. New York: Henry Holt and Company, LLC, 2009.

First Break All the Rules: What the World's Greatest Managers Do Differently, Marcus Buckingham and Curt Coffman. New York: Simon & Schuster, 1999.

The First 90 Days, Michael Watkins, Boston: Harvard Business School Publishing, 2003.

The Five Most Important Questions You Will Ever Ask About Your Organization, Peter F. Drucker with James Collins, Philip Kotler, James Kouzes, Judith Rodin, V. Kasturi Rangan, and Frances Hesselbein. San Francisco: Josey-Bass, 2008.

Little Bets: How Breakthrough Ideas Emerge From Small Discoveries, Peter Sims. New York: Simon & Schuster, 2011.

The Orange Revolution: How One Great Team Can Transform An Entire Organization, Adrian Gostick and Chester Elton. New York: Simon & Schuster, 2011.

Organizational Change:

The Accelerating Organization: Embracing the Human Face of Change, by Arun Maira and Peter B. Scott-Morgan. 1996. McGraw-Hill. Teaches new principles of managing people, teams and organizations, including change-management policies. Addresses technological change.

Agent of Change: My Life, My Practice, by Richard Beckhard. 1997. Jossey-Bass. A foremost organizational consultant shares a lifetime of wisdom, outlining his principles of practice regarding change.

Better Change: Best Practices for Transforming Your Organization, by the Price Waterhouse Change Integration Team. 1994. McGraw-Hill. Toolkit, with much practical advice, giving you the "feel" of change projects.

Beyond the Wall of Resistance: Unconventional Strategies That Build Support for Change, by Rick Maurer. 1996. Bard. How managers can transform resistance to change into a positive force.

Breaking Free: A Prescription for Personal and Organizational Change, by David M. Noer. 1997. Jossey-Bass. Offers practical steps for succeeding in the modern workplace and encourages workers to let of the familiar and look toward a self-directed future with excitement.

Champions of Change: How CEOs and Their Companies are Mastering the Skills of Radical Change, by David A. Nadler. 1997. Jossey-Bass. Sometimes you have to reexamine the status quo and make drastic changes in the way you do business. This book shows you how others met the challenge.

Changing the Way We Change: Gaining Control of Major Operational Change, by Jeanenne LaMarsh. 1995. Addison Wesley. Provides the necessar y tools to implement successful change in the engineering processes of manufacturing companies.

Chicken Soup for the Soul at Work: 101 Stories of Courage, Compassion, and Creativity in the Workplace, by Jack Canfield, Martin Rutte, et al. 1996. Health Communications. Encourages creativity in the workplace. Competing for the Future, by Gary Hamel and C.K. Prahalad. 1996. Harvard Business. Complacent managers who get too comfortable will see their businesses fall behind.

Corporate Hyenas at Work!: How to Spot and Outwit Them by Being Hyenawise, by Susan Marais-Steinman and Magriet Herman. 1997. Kagiso. Looks at issues of disempowerment of workers, and how they can help themselves by healing the workplace.

The Corporate Mystic: A Guidebook for Visionaries with Their Feet on the Ground, by Gay Hendricks and Kate Ludeman. 1997. Bantam. Offers solutions to everyday work problems including giving and receiving feedback, ending destructive turf battles, handling losses, etc.

Deep Change: Discovering the Leader Within (Jossey-Bass Business and Management Series), by Robert E. Quinn. 1996. Jossey-Bass. How all employees can be agents of change in corporate environments.

The Human Side of Change: A Practical Guide to Organization Redesign (Jossey-Bass Business and Management Series), by Timothy J. Galpin. 1996. Jossey-Bass. Focuses on the behaviors needed to effect change: forming teams, developing leadership, measuring performance, providing feedback, etc.

Leading Change, by John P. Kotter. 1996. Harvard Business School Press. Author suggests that change strategies often fail because the changes don't alter behavior within the corporation. Outlines an eight step process for establishing a sense of urgency.

Leading from the Heart: Choosing Courage over Fear in the Workplace, by Kay Gilley.1996. Butterworth-Heinemann. Playing by the rules doesn't always work, not in corporate life anyway. Learn to feel safe through personal accountability.

Making a Difference: Strategies and Tools for Transforming Your Organization, by Bruce C. Nixon. 1998. AMACOM. Provides the tools for challenging tradition and implementing visionary change. Includes a discussion of welcoming divergence and diversity.

The Manager's Tool Kit: Practical Tips for Tackling 100 On-the-Job Problems, by Cy Charney. 1995. AMACOM. - Covers everything from benchmarking to conflict resolution to project management.

Management Would Be Easy...If It Weren't for the People: A Guide to Managing People More Effectively by Understanding the Basic Principles of Psychology, by Patricia J. Addesso. 1996. AMACOM. - Helps managers improve communication, reduce conflict, etc.

Managing the Change Process: A Fieldbook for Change Agents, Team Leaders, and Reengineering Managers, by David K. Carr, Kelvin J. Hard, and William J. Trahant. 1996. McGraw-Hill. - Practical, proactive tools for managers to ensure the success of their turnaround efforts.

The New Pioneers: The Men and Women Who Are Transforming the Workplace and Marketplace, by Thomas Petzinger. 1999. Simon & Schuster. - Profiles people who dared to think about abandoning old paradigms of doing business.

People Styles at Work: Making Bad Relationships Good and Good Relationships Better, by Robert Bolton and Dorothy Grover Bolton. 1996. AMACOM. - Overcome personality conflicts by understanding other people's differences.

Sacred Cows Make the Best Burgers: Developing Change-Ready People and Organizations, by Robert J. Kriegel and David Brandt. 1997. Warner Books. - Reveals why people in organizations hold on to the old, and how to inspire them to change. Shows you how to coach yourself and others.

Beyond Corporate Transformation: A Whole Systems Approach to Creating and Sustaining High Performance, by Christopher W. Head. 1997. Productivity Press. - Employees resist change when they don't understand the changes, don't see the benefit of those changes, and are uninvolved in the process.

Personal Change: The Seven Habits of Highly Effective People: Powerful Lessons in Personal Change, by Stephen R. Covey. 1990. Fireside.- Business bestseller, this book is a manual for performing better professionally and personally. Also available on cassette.

The Caterpillar Doesn't Know: How Personal Change Is Creating Organizational Change, by Kenneth R. Hey and Peter D. Moore. 1998. Free Press. - Provides clear insights, through examples, into how enlightened leaders are using their own personal changes to restructure their companies.

Getting Out from Under: Redefining Your Priorities in an Overwhelming World: A Powerful Program for Personal Change, by Stephanie Winston. 1999. Perseus Books. - A program for making meaningful change in our lives, helping readers to prioritize and organize.

Profit from Experience: A Handbook for Learning, Growth, and Change, by Michael J. O'Brien and Larry Shook. 1998. Berkley. - Improve your outlook, habits, and patterns of behavior to increase personal effectiveness in any task you choose to take on.

Success Is Not An Accident: Change Your Choice, Change Your Life, by Tommy Newberry. 1997. Looking Glass Books. - Practical suggestions for getting the most from yourself personally and professionally.

Turning Feedback into Change: 31 Principles for Managing Personal Development Through Feedback, by Joe Folkman. 1996. Novations. - From on expert on feedback systems.

Changing Your Spots: A Guide to Personal Change, by Terry Wilson. 1998. Gower. - Helps you understand the process of personal change, and how it can alter your life.

Choosing Joy: Change Your Life for the Better, by Gary Null, Vicki Riba Koestler. 1998. Carroll & Graf. - Clear and simple suggestions for making long lasting, positive changes in your life, focusing on health and general well-being.

Leadership Transitions Solutions **Services**

Leadership Transitions Solutions is dedicated to nourishing the ability to learn in leaders at every level. We see the ability to learn as a crucial competency for leaders in contemporary organizations where incessant change is the norm. Transition events and performance challenges are unrivalled opportunities for learning and for increasing the ability to learn.

- Our **FastStart™** application ensures a successful beginning for any manager facing the challenge of a new assignment. **FastStart™** provides the manager with a comprehensive assessment of the new organization based on interviews with leaders, peers, direct reports and customers. The interviews are efficiently conducted by way of **Dialogue™**, a web-based application that summarizes the interview responses to produce the organizational assessment. The assessment identifies the key challenges facing the new manager and provides the foundation for an effective action plan for the first 100 days in the new job. The action plan is developed by the manager with consulting support from a Transition Coach. The benefits of this Program are:

  - Identifies the specific challenges inherent in the new role by conducting a comprehensive organizational assessment generated by online interviews with Superiors, Peers, Customers and Direct Reports.

  - Captures the intelligence contained in the organizational assessment for immediate use by the new leader.

  - Speeds up the integration of the new leader with his/her team by efficiently providing detailed personal and professional information introducing each team member, while identifying their perspectives and concerns related to key organizational issues.

170

- Prevents the productivity decline frequently associated with leadership transitions in an organizational unit.

- Supports the leader in the development of an effective action plan for the first 100 days in the new role.

- Provides an empirical basis for follow up coaching support.

- Provides data on individual performance that can be mined to produce actionable intelligence related to overall leadership development needs without violating the confidentiality of individual responses.

- Our **FreshStart™** application is for managers who are struggling in their current role. The Fresh Start™ application is designed to gather feedback for individual managers facing difficulty in their current assignment, not performing at the necessary level or facing challenges that threaten their ability to maintain required performance levels. The struggling leader requires the ability to adopt new perspectives and to eliminate the blind spots affecting current performance. Leaders facing challenges that threaten their performance need insight into the changes they need to make to maintain effective performance. As with the FAST START™ application for the new leader, we use a structured methodology to gather feedback for the struggling leader. The information comes from their leaders, peers, customers and direct reports. With the support of a personal coach the struggling leader uses the feedback to construct a personal development plan with metrics which ensure a return to effective performance.

The Summary Report generated by Fresh Start™ responses is a powerful complement to typical online 360 degree feedback programs due to its exclusive focus on specific behaviors related to performance improvement. The benefits of this Program are:

- Identifies the perception of individual leadership effectiveness on the part of Superiors, Peers, Customers and Direct Reports

171

in relation to performance within specific dimensions of the current job through online interviews.

- Captures the feedback for immediate use by the leader.

- Provides follow up coaching support to enhance the learning available in the feedback results.

- Enables the participant to enhance individual strengths and address development needs within the current job.

- Provides data on individual performance that can be mined to produce actionable intelligence related to overall leadership development needs without violating the confidentiality of individual responses.

Leadership Team Fitness Inventory (LTFI): The LTFI is an opportunity for a leader to take the pulse of his/her team and identify stretch opportunities that will enhance team performance in measurable ways. The Inventory consists of two confidential, web-based interviews:

- An Organization Review that identifies policies and practices that are working and not working and elicits recommendations from the team for specific improvements. The review also reveals whether there is clarity and consensus regarding the vision driving the organization.

- A Team Dynamics Inquiry that identifies how well the team is functioning around five key
Characteristics of high-performing teams:

- Trust

- Commitment

- Conflict Management

- Accountability

- Attention to Detail

- Results of the interviews are summarized and form the basis of an agenda for a team meeting facilitated by one of our coaches. The meeting produces a team action plan for the coming year. The benefits of this Program are:

172

- Identifies team dynamics in relation to trust, conflict, commitment, accountability and attention to results.

- Captures the team feedback for immediate use by the leader.

- Educates the leader in regard to team dynamics and the art of developing and leading a team toward high performance.

- Provides an empirical basis for coaching both the team leader and the team.

- Provides data on individual performance that can be mined to produce actionable information related to overall leadership development needs without violating the confidentiality of individual responses.

- Provides an opportunity to make the core values of the organization those of individual teams.

Myers-Briggs Type Indicator (MBTI) Workshops: The MBTI is a useful tool that often adds useful information to the **FastStart™**, FreshStart™ and LTFI Programs. When managers have a clear grasp of their operating style and its strengths and weaknesses, they are better able to determine developmental strategies to address specific issues.

Executive Coaching: All of our services are accompanied by coaching support from our experienced team of coaches. We are available for and frequently asked to provide general coaching support unrelated to any of the programs described above. The benefits of coaching are:

- Enhancement of individual learning from the online feedback gathered in each of the four learning experiences

- Opportunity for confidential exploration of issues identified in the feedback and the development of deeper understanding of personal development needs

- A chance to learn coaching skills for personal use as a leader from a Master coach

www.ingramcontent.com/pod-product-compliance
Lightning Source LLC
Chambersburg PA
CBHW072033190526
45165CB00017B/529

9 7 8 1 4 6 3 6 4 7 3 7 7